T0233837

Lecture Notes
in Business Information Processing   **245**

Series Editors

Wil van der Aalst
Eindhoven Technical University, Eindhoven, The Netherlands
John Mylopoulos
University of Trento, Povo, Italy
Michael Rosemann
Queensland University of Technology, Brisbane, QLD, Australia
Michael J. Shaw
University of Illinois, Urbana-Champaign, IL, USA
Clemens Szyperski
Microsoft Research, Redmond, WA, USA

More information about this series at http://www.springer.com/series/7911

Michael Felderer · Felix Piazolo
Wolfgang Ortner · Lars Brehm
Hans-Joachim Hof (Eds.)

Innovations in Enterprise Information Systems Management and Engineering

4th International Conference, ERP Future 2015 - Research
Munich, Germany, November 16–17, 2015
Revised Papers

 Springer

Editors
Michael Felderer
Institute of Computer Science
University of Innsbruck
Innsbruck
Austria

Felix Piazolo
Andrassy University Budapest
Budapest
Hungary

Wolfgang Ortner
FH JOANNEUM – University of Applied
   Sciences
Graz
Austria

Lars Brehm
University of Applied Sciences Munich
Munich
Germany

Hans-Joachim Hof
University of Applied Sciences Munich
Munich
Germany

ISSN 1865-1348   ISSN 1865-1356   (electronic)
Lecture Notes in Business Information Processing
ISBN 978-3-319-32798-3   ISBN 978-3-319-32799-0   (eBook)
DOI 10.1007/978-3-319-32799-0

Library of Congress Control Number: 2016935972

© Springer International Publishing Switzerland 2016
This work is subject to copyright. All rights are reserved by the Publisher, whether the whole or part of the material is concerned, specifically the rights of translation, reprinting, reuse of illustrations, recitation, broadcasting, reproduction on microfilms or in any other physical way, and transmission or information storage and retrieval, electronic adaptation, computer software, or by similar or dissimilar methodology now known or hereafter developed.
The use of general descriptive names, registered names, trademarks, service marks, etc. in this publication does not imply, even in the absence of a specific statement, that such names are exempt from the relevant protective laws and regulations and therefore free for general use.
The publisher, the authors and the editors are safe to assume that the advice and information in this book are believed to be true and accurate at the date of publication. Neither the publisher nor the authors or the editors give a warranty, express or implied, with respect to the material contained herein or for any errors or omissions that may have been made.

Printed on acid-free paper

This Springer imprint is published by Springer Nature
The registered company is Springer International Publishing AG Switzerland

Preface

This book contains revised papers from the 2015 ERP Future — Research Conference, held in Munich, Germany, in November 2015. The 12 papers presented in this volume were carefully peer-reviewed and selected from a total of 23 submissions.

The ERP Future — Research Conference is a platform for research in ERP systems and closely related topics such as business processes, business intelligence, and enterprise information systems. Submitted contributions cover the given topics from a business and a technological point of view with high theoretical as well as practical impact.

February 2016

Michael Felderer
Felix Piazolo
Wolfgang Ortner
Lars Brehm
Hans-Joachim Hof

Organization

Program Committee

Martin Adam	University of Applied Sciences Kufstein, Austria
Rogerio Atem de Carvalho	Instituto Federal Fluminense, Brazil
Dagmar Auer	Johannes Kepler University Linz, Austria
Irene Barba Rodriguez	University of Seville, Spain
Josef Bernhart	EURAC Bozen/Bolzano, Italy
Götz Botterweck	Lero - The Irish Software Engineering Research Centre, Ireland
Ruth Breu	University of Innsbruck, Austria
Oliver Christ	ZHAW Zurich University of Applied Sciences, Switzerland
Jörg Courant	HTW Berlin, Germany
Maya Daneva	University of Twente, The Netherlands
Dirk Draheim	Software Competence Center Hagenberg, Austria
Jörg Dörr	Fraunhofer IESE, Germany
Sandy Eggert	Berlin School of Economics and Law, Germany
Kerstin Fink	University of Applied Sciences Salzburg, Austria
Kai Fischbach	University of Bamberg, Germany
Johann Gamper	Free University of Bozen-Bolzano, Italy
Norbert Gronau	University of Potsdam, Germany
Hans H. Hinterhuber	University of Innsbruck, Austria
Sami Jantunen	Lappeenranta University of Technology, Finland
Reinhold Karner	Universität Innsbruck, Austria
Asmamaw Mengistie	Sholla Computing, USA
David Meyer	University of Applied Sciences, Technikum Wien, Austria
Wolfgang Ortner	FH JOANNEUM — University of Applied Sciences, Austria
Lukas Paa	Andrassy University Budapest, Hungary
Kurt Promberger	University of Innsbruck, Austria
Friedrich Roithmayr	Johannes Kepler University Linz, Austria
Matthias Schumann	University of Göttingen, Germany
Stéphane S. Somé	University of Ottawa, Canada
Alfred Taudes	WU — Vienna University of Economics and Business, Austria
Victoria Torres Bosch	Polytechnic University of Valencia, Spain

Contents

Education in Enterprise Systems

erp4students: Introducing a Best Practice Example for Vocational Training in Universities

Thomas Richter[✉], Heimo H. Adelsberger, Pouyan Khatami, and Taymaz Khatami

University of Duisburg-Essen, Universitätsstr. 9, 45141 Essen, Germany
{thomas.richter,heimo.adelsberger,
pouyan.khatami,taymaz.khatami}@uni-due.de

Abstract. In this paper, we introduce the international program *erp4students* as general example on how to successfully prepare university students for the world of works without having to give up the basic principle in higher education, i.e., to exclusively provide sustainable education. We start with introducing the basic concept and design of the program and provide information regarding the demographic development over the past decade and implemented quality assurance mechanisms. Subsequently, the scope and design of and hitherto achieved insights from the Learning Culture Survey are outlined. On the basis of found results, we finally discuss how *erp4students* can deal with possible culture-specific issues that latest might emerge when the program gets available for learners in the Asian context.

Keywords: Enterprise Resource Planning · E-Learning · Higher education · SAP · International study program · Vocational training · Culture

1 Introduction

Since many years, industry has been complaining that students, leaving the universities, are full of theoretical knowledge which is not or just partly applicable in their future jobs. The graduates often would completely lack relevant competences and soft skills, working practice, and even the most basic understanding of what business-life is alike. This critique from the world of works towards academia is so basic that it could actually go back to the roots of academia when universities were established and started to provide higher education. Academia's answer, however, might have been the same even then: Every (academic) university's task is to provide a profound level of understanding of general and thus, timeless concepts, theories, ideas, and mechanisms – and even beyond that: of life, existence, the world, its entities, and the interactions amongst the entities. In contrast, applied knowledge and, particularly, application-related knowledge were considered timely restricted and to latter, even "short-termed". As compromises, technical universities and universities of applied sciences were created in the German (language) context which focused on applied knowledge (if not on application-related knowledge).

One of the major tasks for the context of Higher Education that derived from Bologna and the Sorbonne declaration was the general idea to initially prepare students for the

© Springer International Publishing Switzerland 2016
M. Felderer et al. (Eds.): ERP Future 2015 - Research, LNBIP 245, pp. 3–18, 2016.
DOI: 10.1007/978-3-319-32799-0_1

world of works: When granting Bachelor degrees after three to four years of studying, universities should ensure that the knowledge and understanding of the graduates makes them valuable enough for being employed in a firm. In Germany, Bologna failed due to several reasons: First, Bachelor and Master degrees substituted the well-known and highly valued traditional German Diploma and Magister degrees: Even though they actually constituted a far higher level, enterprises simply understood the Bachelor degrees as the traditional halfway examinations of the former diploma degrees. Second, the government did not sufficiently support the implementation by promoting the newly established degrees and their potential for the enterprises. Third, as the most problematic issue, in a century-old tradition, the German language countries already had established a practical tertiary education, the apprenticeships in industry-related and crafting disciplines. To some extent, the Bachelor-degree constituted a concurrent type of education (in both directions) [1]. Apprenticeships, be it as programmers, chefs, nurses, metal workers, painters, wood-crafters, mechanics, electricians, mechatronics, or biological-, information- and chemical-technical assistants took three to three-and-a-half years and were carried out in both, enterprises and public schools; latter were responsible for the theoretical foundation and ensured that apprentices from very specialized enterprises (e.g., learning to cook within a Chinese restaurant) received the full set of competences to complete general job-related tasks in any professional context (cooking in any type of kitchen). Such apprenticeships also included application-related knowledge. Bachelors of craft or industry were much better prepared for immediately being assigned to concrete practical tasks in the enterprises even if not fully understanding in detail why something is to be done in a particular way (e.g., never fighting burning fat with water!). As for the academic Bachelor-degree holders, they are expected to adopt themselves to any task within a limited amount of time (just not immediately). Thus, in the German language context, the non-academic (practical) Bachelor degree from the Chamber of Crafts or the Chamber of Industry and Commerce is in direct concurrence to thematically related academic Bachelor degrees – with a clear advantage for the apprenticeships.

It is still not fully clear which specific abilities distinguish academic Bachelor degree holders from non-academic bachelors in terms of advantages on the job market at entry-level. Sure, academic Bachelors have a deep general understanding of the context and above that, also a basic understanding of typical strategies, measures, and theories, which the former apprentices lack to a large extent. Just, at least for the first years of employment, the return of investment – when employing the cheaper non-academic bachelors who far quicker can fully be integrated within current work processes – still appears higher for the enterprises. In a yet unpublished study we conducted some years ago on the acceptance of Bachelor degrees for employment in German firms, we found that German enterprises rather employ alumni with an old Diploma or a new Master degree in Information Systems than with an academic Bachelor degree from the same field. The major reason for related perceptions of the Bachelor degree holders were said to be a missing argument why they should earn a higher salary without granting a higher return on investment (in the first years) than the "apparently" adequate non-academic bachelors. We additionally found that on a rather general level, the human resources managers we interviewed were quite unaware what a Bachelor degree actually would mean in their specific fields.

The central question to answer is: What can universities do to better prepare their students for the world of works without having to betray their basic principles of education? In this paper, the program *erp4students* is being introduced as a best-practice example on how the gap can be bridged between the fully sustainable provision of general theoretical knowledge (the traditional academic educational approach) and the very particular demands from the world of works for applied and application-related knowledge and competences (see http://www.erp4students.eu).

After the introduction of the state of the art, we first describe the basic ideas and concepts behind the program. Subsequently, we introduce the particular program- and course design, hitherto made achievements, and demographic data on the program's development from the last decade. For further expanding the geographical accessibility of the program, particularly towards the Asian context, our most current research results from the Learning Culture Survey (LCS) suggested that a redesign might be helpful regarding some issues. With the LCS, we investigate culture-specific expectations, perceptions, and attitudes of university students. This comparative research shall (a) generally lead to a better understanding of the impact of Culture in Education, (b) help preventing intercultural conflicts by supporting educators in creating culture-sensible course designs, and finally (3) support educators and learners during their preparation phases when going or teaching classes abroad. In order to link both, the program *erp4students* and the LCS, we briefly introduce the LCS and its most relevant key findings, and afterwards, transfer the found results to recommendations for being considered in *erp4students*. Finally, we introduce our plans for the future as well as issues that still require solutions.

2   University and Professional Training: No Contradiction

With the *erp4students* project, the university of Duisburg-Essen (UDE) demonstrates that it is actually possible to bridge the gap between the traditional view on academic education and the enterprises, which expect recent graduates having very concrete practice-related competences. It appears that two worlds would crash in each other when sustainably teaching timeless knowledge (focusing on general methods and theories) has to result in abilities currently relevant for present-day key-technologies and applications which might already turn irrelevant after a very limited time. *erp4students* has been designed as an offer to university students for extra-curricular professional training. In this sense, the courses in *erp4students* are not designed as integral parts of any particular study program, but they are offered to being voluntarily taken in addition to, e.g., the more general courses on methods and theories in Enterprise Resource Planning and Supply Chain Management in our BIS-Master program. Without defining preconditions regarding foreknowledge and picking up the learners on a very low level of IT knowledge, *erp4students* is even open to students from all study fields. While, at first in 2006, *erp4students* exclusively was available in German language and to German students in the field of Information Systems Research, nowadays, students from many countries and diverse fields of study have access to the courses in up to four languages, can participate in examinations, and achieve the provided highly valued certifications to prove their ability in using and programming SAP systems.

Without excluding the theoretical understanding of the field, the educational program *erp4students* offers learners the opportunity to intensively engage with practical aspects of Enterprise Resource Planning (ERP). In today's world of work where just a little percentage of enterprises remains without the support of Information Technology, understanding and to know how to deal with ERP systems is fundamental for a big part of the work force. However, the program does not limit the learned lessons to an in-depth understanding of the underlying theoretical concepts and mechanisms of ERP, but it leads the students through many hands-on sessions to achieve practice-relevant competences in working with the world's leading ERP software, which, with a market-share of 24 percentage (2013), is the solution of the SAP SE [2].

With the SAP University Alliance as a strong partner at the side, *erp4students* provides a set of extra-curricular courses, developed at the University Duisburg-Essen in Germany, exclusively offered to university students (non-profit).

Writing a steadily ongoing success story, *erp4students* offers a growing number of practice-oriented, student-focused, purely Internet-based, and tutor-supported courses on different functions of ERP systems. In 2006, when *erp4students* launched its first basic SAP-course in German language, 63 courses were booked, successfully finalized, and eventually awarded with university certificates. In the launching year, all participants came from Germany. Today, ten years later, students from 110 countries booked 5200 courses. The learners are actively participating in both their course-work and community building and permanently supported by tutors. Figure 1 shows today's available thirteen qualified courses on beginner and advanced level *erp4students* currently offers. Most of the courses are available in German and English and some, additionally, in Spanish and Russian. Courses on advanced level presume the knowledge from the courses on beginner-level.

Issue	Course Content	Languages
SAP ERP	Integrated Business Processes with SAP ERP (TERP10)	DE, EN, ES, RU
	SAP ERP Customizing I (Beginner)	DE, EN, ES
	SAP ERP Customizing II (Advanced)	DE, EN
	Introduction to Enterprise Resource Planning	EN
SAP BW	SAP BW I (Beginner)	DE, EN, ES
	SAP BW II (Advanced Business Intelligence)	DE, EN
	SAP BO - SAP BusinessObjects and SAP HANA	DE, EN
	Data Warehousing (Beginner)	EN
SAP CRM	SAP CRM (Beginner)	DE, EN
SAP PPS	SAP Productions planning und control I (Beginner)	DE
	SAP Productions planning und control II (Advanced)	DE
ABAP	ABAP I (Beginner)	DE, EN
	ABAP II (Advanced)	DE, EN

Fig. 1. Today's courses within the program *erp4students*

The workload of each course is approx. 180 h – this workload corresponds to six ECTS points (European Credit Transfer System) or four credits (U.S. credit system). In addition to the university certificate (pass/fail), the students have the opportunity to participate in official consultant certification exam offered by the SAP SE to a reduced cost.

The whole process students undergo from registration to certification is outlined in Fig. 2. Due to its widely linear and homogenous (the same process for all courses) design, it is easy to cope with for the learners so that they always know where they stand and what they have to do next.

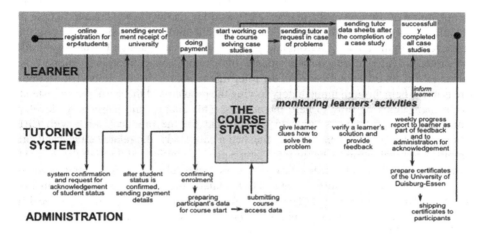

Fig. 2. *erp4students* – The overall process model

The whole process can be subdivided into three distinct sets of sub-processes, i.e.:

1. the registration, including the transmission of relevant personal data, the choice of a course, and completing the payment procedure;
2. the course itself, starting with the dark field in the lower middle, fully supported by local tutors (assigned in the separate middle block);
3. and finally, the formalities to grant and deliver the certificates.

The whole process is implemented as a dialogue between the student (in the upper frame), the tutoring system (in the middle frame), and the administration of *erp4students* (in the lower frame).

The first set of sub-processes is initialized by the online registration of a student. At this point, the student has already decided for a particular course he/she is interested in. Within a defined period at the beginning of each semester, a student submits the completed online registration form (to be found on the website of *erp4students*) to the administration and in return, receives a confirmation alongside with an information package and the request for an acknowledgement of the legal status as a student. The student-status is the only mandatory condition to participate. After the interested student has submitted the enrolment receipt of the university he/she is currently studying at, the *erp4students* administration confirms the student's meeting of all formal requirements and submits the payment details. The student, in return, initiates the payment. Once completed, the administration confirms the formal enrolment and welcomes the new participant. However, all registered learners begin with their course work at the same time and have the same deadline for completion.

After the administration sent the access data for the course via E-Mail to the participant (in the following, "learner") which initializes the second set of sub-processes, further communication mainly takes place between the learner and the *erp4students* tutoring system. The tutoring system, as an entity represented in the middle frame of Fig. 2, actually consists of individuals and teams of real persons who permanently monitor the students' activities in order to quickly provide support in case of need. In the beginning of this phase, the learner starts working on the chosen course. In case of difficulties that appear to overburden the learner, the tutor can be contacted using the online forum in the course environment, or more individual, through E-Mail. Assumed the learner provided all relevant details, the tutor returns clues in order to support the learner to find an own solution; else, the tutor might ask for more details. The strategy here is not to help through immediately solving the problems of the learners, but instead, giving them clues on how to help themselves. This enables the learners to develop competences for problem solving in general and for the practical work with ERP systems, in particular. When a learner finished a case study, the related data sheets are submitted for evaluation to the tutor (an active process, initialized through the learner). In the next step, the tutor verifies the correctness of the delivered solution and provides feedback regarding its quality. If the solution actually meets the defined requirements, the case study is being closed. The successful completion is included in the weekly progress report, which the tutor submits to both the learner – as a part of the constant feedback – and the administration for purposes of documentation.

Once a learner has successfully completed all case studies within the course, the last set of sub-processes is initialized: First, the tutoring system informs learner and administration of this new status quo. Subsequently, the administration prepares the certificate of the University of Duisburg-Essen and ships it to the learner.

By means of our certificate, a student can prove being in command of the theoretical knowledge as well as having successfully mastered all practical case studies of the course. The certificate of the University of Duisburg-Essen additionally enables students to ask their own university administration to recognize the achievements for their own course of study and eventually, is the precondition to register for the official consultant certification exam offered by the SAP SE.

3   Demographic Development of erp4students

The program *erp4students* underwent quite an impressive development from the initial enrolment of a single TERP10 course for 63 local students until today. Both, the numbers of participants and the regional distribution steadily increased over the course of the years between 2006 and today, 2015.

3.1 Development of Student-Participant-Numbers over the Years

As the following Fig. 3 shows, the participant numbers of the program *erp4students* steadily increased between 2006 and 2014. As for 2015, there are already 5200 distinct participants registered.

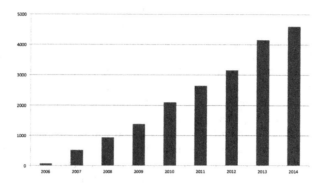

Fig. 3. *erp4students:* development of student numbers from 2006 to 2014

With the wider distribution of the program across the world, our membership in the Academy Cube initialized by the SAP SE, and with the increasing variety of course modules, we expect the hitherto monitored progress in numbers of participants and regional distribution to be ongoing at least for the next decade.

3.2 Today's Distribution of Learners across Countries

In 2006, *erp4students* consisted of a single course (Introduction to SAP R/3) which was exclusively offered to students of the University of Duisburg-Essen. This year, in 2015, 5200 students from 110 countries and more than 300 different universities are participating in the *erp4students* courses. Figure 4 above shows the distribution of countries in the world where the learners currently come from.

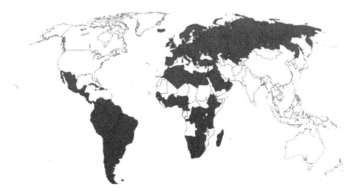

Fig. 4. Distribution of participants across countries in 2015

4   Quality Management in erp4students

A central reason for the success of *erp4students* is that quality assessments are conducted on a regular basis, leading to improvements of the current courses and the design of new courses. The Quality Management strategy within erp4stuents follows the first part of the German concept "Qualitätsplattform Lernen" (transl.: "quality platform learning") [3], which describes a holistic approach basing on three parts, i.e.: 1. quality of educational offers, 2. basic quality of organizations, and 3. measures for excellent quality in organizations. The chosen first part of the concept deals with the request for a transparent provision of information regarding the educational offers, related to clear definitions of target groups and purposes, full transparency regarding the chosen approaches for didactics and methodology, used media, implemented roles, tasks for each of the roles, measures to control learning success, technological issues, and evaluation. Several national and international standards have been united within this particular approach.

While most QM-instruments are implemented and just used once during course planning and production, the student evaluation is used repeatedly for ongoing quality control. An important aspect of *erp4students* is the orientation on the needs of the learners in a complex laboratory like setting; every improvement potential is evaluated and – if found helpful – is implemented in the courses in the next semester. The most important tool in this process is an online questionnaire. The survey is conducted at the end of each semester; the students are asked to evaluate a small number of questions on a 7-point Likert scale from −3 (very bad) to +3 (excellent).

4.1   Student Evaluation: Focus and Criteria

The following thirteen questions constitute the part of the questionnaire which directly deals with the perception of the course's quality and ideas for improvements. The first ten questions were adopted from the quality management questionnaire as it is implemented for and established within the virtual study program "VAWi", an e-Learning-based BIS-Master program. The subsequent three questions of the following list were exclusively (and additionally) developed for the context of *erp4students*.

Students' Questionnaire (excerpt):
1. How would you evaluate the mediation of teaching contents?
2. How would you evaluate the usefulness of the contents for your original field of study?
3. How would you evaluate the usefulness of the contents for your future job?
4. How would you evaluate the structuring of the contents?
5. How would you evaluate the comprehensibility of the contents?
6. How would you evaluate the quality of learning support?
7. How would you evaluate the general organizing of your course?
8. How would you evaluate the quality of support in case of organizational issues?
9. How would you evaluate the quality of support in case of technical issues?
10. How would you evaluate the communication with your peers?

11. Would you rather wish to work on a platform of the type like Facebook or StudiVZ which could be used to support communication with peers and enterprises?
12. Do you plan to participate in further courses of *erp4students'* portfolio?
13. Do you plan to recommend *erp4students* to your friends and peers?

4.2 Example for Results of Learners' Evaluation: Winter Semester 2014/2015

The average item results of the thirteen questions found in the latest evaluation are displayed in Fig. 5. The items in the bar graphs exactly follow the sequence of questions listed in Sect. 4.1. As direct feedback from the learners, this evaluation is a crucial input for the improvement of the program. As another quality measure, particularly for the tutoring services, the tutors directly receive feedback from the learners, e.g. via E-Mail, in chats and the forum, or via telephone. This feedback is collected over the course of the semester, and together with the tutors' own observations during the courses' runtime, it serves as input for later team discussions.

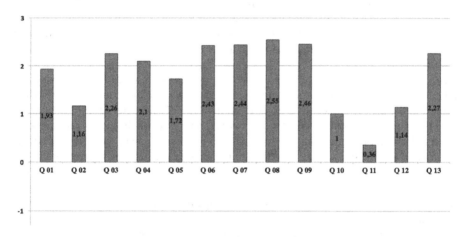

Fig. 5. Results of learner evaluation for *erp4students*

In the winter semester 2014/2015, we invited the 2146 registered learners to complete our online questionnaire. Eventually, a total of n = 295 completed questionnaires were returned (13.75 % participation rate). The averages for all of the questions were to be found at the positive side of the scale! A distinction between the origins of the respondents did not yet take place in that evaluation round.

The evaluation of both, the perceived quality of contents and services, generally revealed very positive in the average (above +1.5). Even though still positive, some lower evaluations encourage further discussion.

Within the items 2 and 3, the learners evaluated the usefulness of the courses for (2) their current field of study and (3) their future job. While a significantly lower amount of students assigned a direct relationship to (and thus, benefit for) their current study efforts in their university, most students assigned a high level of relevance regarding their future jobs. We understand this result as a confirmation that *erp4students* actually supports the learners with contents that are not considered during their regular studies. It additionally shows that learners enter our program from fields that are not even linked to the courses' core disciplines Information Technology and Information Systems. Obviously, learners recognize a relevance of the offered courses for their specific future area and level of employment.

Item 7 refers to the general organizing of the courses. While *erp4students* technically offers several supportive measures embedded in the used platform (like an archive for already passed contents and a calendar function) and additionally provides recommendations for the time management, any decision how to make use of this offer is up to the learners. As found in the Learning Culture Survey, which is being introduced later on, students in some countries generally prefer a more guided teaching style than students from others [4]. Particularly between Western and Eastern countries, such different perceptions of individuality and needs for personal support were monitored. We expect related cultural differences being one reason for the result in the evaluation of this item. The issue is being further monitored in order to improve our services and the perceived "happiness" of our students. We believe that happiness is a highly relevant driver for learner satisfaction and thus, responsible to preserve the initial motivation in education. Investigations on happiness are subject of a quite young research field in the context of economy [5, 6].

The evaluation of Item 10 refers to the communication between the learners. The actual work in the courses, which mainly is related to reading course materials and completing the practical case studies, is to be individually done by each of the participants. Didactical elements like group tasks and group work have, so far, not been considered for implementation; in *erp4students*, no deadlines are defined apart of the start and end date of the course. This design is meant to provide the maximum level of flexibility for the students. For the communication amongst the students, *erp4students* provides a forum. The learners are encouraged to first share their problems (and possible solutions) with peers in order to let others participate in the learning process and eventually, the found solutions. In terms of problem solving, the learners shall just directly involve the tutors, if the peers cannot jointly find an adequate solution. Regarding the quality of such solutions, tutors permanently monitor the forum, moderate when discussion stands still, and intervene if a discussion moves into the wrong direction. However, some students just have a very limited time frame for the completion of their courses and thus, require immediate support from the tutors. Additionally, in some cultures, tutor-support generally is considered to have a higher quality than peer-support, and showing peers weaknesses like the lack of understanding, is considered unacceptable behavior. In the context of *erp4students*, it is yet unclear to which extent either cultural or individual preferences influence the learners' social attitudes and the frequency of their postings within the forum. We will further monitor the issue.

Item 11 is related to a possible redirecting of the *erp4student* service offers. It asks the learners if they would prefer the *erp4students*-platform to rather focus on social networking, providing functionalities as commonly known from Facebook or the German student-portal StudiVZ [7]. With an average 0.36, the answers of the learners were rather indifferent. We learned from these responses that the students appear to follow a very specific purpose when booking our courses, which does not necessarily include peer-to-peer communication or any form of socializing. As consequence, we currently do not plan to implement further opportunities for social networking and/or peer-to-peer communication. However, particularly in terms of social interaction, our current learners' perceptions might not reflect the needs of future Asian students. In case of an expansion of *erp4students* to the Asian context, the implementation of additional social functionalities might still turn out to be helpful for the students' happiness and thus, necessary to implement.

Item 12 again confirms our assumption that the students select distinct courses with a very specific purpose and that the workload of the courses is perceived massive enough not to fall into a "certificate-collection-fever" like monitored in other programs. Our learners are fully happy and justified proud that they successfully managed to complete the chosen courses. Anyways, particularly in cases where students passed a beginner course where an advanced course is available, we expect planned repetitive participations.

5   Culture in Education: The Learning Culture Survey

Our preparations of the Learning Culture Survey started in 2008 with the aim to make the influences of Learning Culture better understandable. We understand "Culture" as a set of perceptions, expectations, attitudes and artifacts, which are typical for people living within a specific society and necessary for its maintenance. While in our context, "Culture in Education" is understood as anything linking both issues, "Learning Culture" is a set of society-specific phenomena related to expectations, perceptions, and attitudes of learners (and directed to education).

With a better understanding of Learning Culture, educators can design learning contents and measures more culture-sensible in order to preserve the learner's initial motivation. We found that its applicability is not limited to but particularly relevant in the field of Technology Enhanced Learning. In this context, educators can hardly recognize in time when students start losing their motivation because mimics and gestures as central indicators to communicate feelings are not available [8].

The Learning Culture Survey uses a method mix approach with a Likert-scale based multilingual questionnaire on Learning Culture as the central instrument for data collection. Further yet, applied qualitative measures were monitoring, conducting different types of interviews, and action research; all together serve to find explanations for the results from the quantitative investigation.

Investigations within the Learning Culture Survey mainly focus on the context of Higher Education whereas in the meantime, also selective investigations were carried out in the context of professional training. The questionnaire covers 102 items from a variety of culture-specific characteristics, which are,

- the perceived roles and assigned tasks of lecturers and tutors,
- perceptions towards feedback and motivation,
- value of, perceptions towards, and attitudes within group work,
- gender related issues, and
- time management.

We (Adelsberger and Richter) started our first comparative investigation in 2010 in the countries Germany and South Korea. These countries were chosen for our initial investigations because Müller et al. reported both countries as the only two available on earth that widely can be considered culturally homogenous [9]. However, we needed answers for some very basic questions. We had serious doubts that the commonly applied theory from value-based culture research would be appropriate within our context of education, as it says that culture generally is a national issue (basing on the concept of a nation's spirit of Montesquieu) and fully transferable to any context within the whole national society [10]. Thus, we investigated if culture-specific results found in investigations the context of Learning Culture in Higher Education might be transferable across different faculties within one university, across same faculties from different universities, across universities in general (as average values) and finally, across educational contexts, which were Professional (In-House) Training and school education. In order to answer our questions, we conducted in-depth investigations in Germany, involving whole student populations from three German universities from different geographical parts of the country. In South Korea, we orally invited students in the streets and in Seoul's subway using a random route algorithm and were able to collect data from 39 different Korean universities. In Germany, further on, we received and analyzed data from two German DAX-noted enterprises where office works were asked to complete a slightly modified version of our questionnaire (for more details please refer to [4, 10, 11]). Even though we recognized a certain spectrum of diversity between all contexts within Higher Education, Learning Culture, in both countries, was found to still being quite homogenous across faculties and across universities. However, we found easily explainable differences in the responses between the contexts Higher Education and Professional Training. We did not additionally investigate the context of K12 education, because the recent studies from Bühler et al. [12] and Mitra et al. [13] already indicated that culture in education appears not to have the same effect or value to children below an age of twelve years than older children. We suspect curiosity being one reason for this difference as it particularly influences decisions and perceptions of younger children. In a later investigation, we collected data within the Higher Education context of French and British Cameroon. Both datasets appeared extremely different. We applied an a-priori/a-posterior analysis and found the datasets distinguished by 99 %. As conclusion, particularly in countries where different societies were force-joined during colonialisation, the concept of a nation-wide culture is not necessarily applicable but instead, more specific investigations are required.

As expected, we found vast differences between the two investigated countries Germany and South Korea. However, in some details, we surprisingly found little diversion; surprisingly, because the comparative culture-related research in economy, sociology, and psychology encouraged very different expectations: While we expected the South Korean (in the following, just "Korean") students having difficulties in dealing with critique but in fact, we found that they expect critique as a part of feedback much more than the German students claimed they would. The expected way to receive feedback (including critique), however, was different. While the German students accepted critique, even if not constructive, in front of their peers, the Korean students strongly prefer to receive it in a more private environment. In terms of group work, massive differences were found regarding several aspects, e.g., which kind of tasks should be best completed in groups, which evaluation strategies should be applied (individual vs. collective), or which criteria usually are applied when groups are to be formed (and who should form the groups). In the context of motivation, in contrast, we just found slight differences in the comparison of the countries' average responses; at least for these two national contexts, many of our state-ments on motivation appear not to touch culture-specific but rather individually different issues. In terms of the perceptions of the roles and tasks of professors and tutors, we again found vast differences. These are implemented as two blocks of statements for each group, professors and tutors. First of all, the Korean students provided almost the same responses in both blocks while the German students' answers were very different. The students of both countries actually knew the concept of tutorials. In subsequently conducted inter-views, we found that the "tutors", in South Korea, mostly are the professors themselves while in Germany, elder students are employed to manage these tasks. Regarding the role of the professors, the Korean students perceived their professors as unfailing and addition-ally assigned the role of a trusted person, which explains why guest students at German universities often struggle when asked to criticize their lecture and its content. We further on found much higher expectations towards services that are to be provided by educators in South Korea than in Germany. Last, as already indicated, professors appear to play a much more personal role for the Korean students than for the German students. In later interviews we found out that in contrast to the German system, private universities in South Korea have a fixed 1:10 quota between full professors and students. At least in theory, new students can only enter a program at a South Korean university, if a full professor is avail-able to support them; else first, a new professor needs to be employed. The quota is to be met on university level so that the relation of 1:10 might not be exactly the same in all faculties but compared to Germany, a far higher level of direct support anyways is possible.

6 Mastering Future Cultural Challenges in erp4students

In *erp4students*, we constantly expanded our regional distribution over the course of the past decade. Apart of applying some translations and offering tutor-support in the languages of the translations, we did not yet take cultural issues into consideration. We, however, expect that latest when we enter the Asian context, it might become necessary because else, we risk to loose students in that contexts.

   In the context of our Learning Culture Survey, we did not yet explicitly investigate learning environments that fully run over the Internet, using ICT as exclusive means for all communication, the distribution of contents, the completion of tasks, examination, and evaluation. Particularly on international level, the Internet community does not necessarily understand the same set of behavioral rules as appropriate as any society does in the physical world. Thus, it is imaginable that the pain threshold of learners using the Internet as means to achieve education strongly differs from what they would consider as demotivating or even as a cultural conflict in the "traditional face-to-face education". In the close future, related investigations are planned to being conducted in the context of *erp4students*.

We already know that if we like to increase our services' availability on a global level, in the long term, we will have to provide translations to and also tutors in more languages. Otherwise, we risk that many students might not be able to join our program because of lacking proficiency in one of the supported languages. Studies from Davis [14] clearly show that language is one of the most significant indicators for culture and the wrong language can constitute a massive barrier for education and business processes. According to Davis [14], a universal language does not even suffice in highly technology-related environments when a '*mutually-meaningful communication link*' is required.

It is not the language alone which might require a redesign: Benavot [15] found that even if educational standards are shared between developing countries, such mutual agreements are limited to, e.g., basic skills in mathematics and problem solving. When it comes to more cognitive aspects of education, pedagogies, and chosen teaching methods, vast differences can be found between the countries.

The culture-specific issues related to group work found in the Learning Culture Survey are not applicable to the context of *erp4students* because the program, at least as it currently is designed, does not include the completion of case studies or any other tasks in group-scenarios. In terms of voluntarily built groups, we expect that Asian students might mingle more than we have experienced from students from other cultures and also, they might rather try to solve issues in groups. For such issues, *erp4students* provides a forum. However, what could lead to a problem is that Asian students might rather focus on tutor support instead of jointly finding solutions with their peers. To some extent such a behavior would undermine our didactical approach but since such demands will not come unexpected, we will be prepared to properly encourage the students in order to try other ways.

An issue we found in the Learning Culture Survey's context-block "Motivation" was related to strategies, students choose to follow when loosing motivation because of too difficult tasks. While German students rather tend to first do the manageable parts and afterwards come back to the difficult ones, Korean students often reported just to solve the manageable parts and completely resign from the more complicated ones. From the German perspective of evaluation, such a behavior would mean a very problematic situation for the tutors. Particularly, when in the end a case study remains uncompleted, it will not be possible to acknowledge the student's efforts with our certificate. A very explicit preparation of the students regarding the general conditions of their course (explicitly related to "what happens, if …") might already help to avoid such cases: If related situations appear imminent, tutors can still intervene and encourage the learners to report their problems.

7   Conclusion and Future Plans

erp4students shows that extra-occupational content offers can sustainably help to implement the Bologna process and support universities (and students) to offer application-related education without having to give up their very basic claim for long-term sustainability. The students, on the other hand, express their need for such opportunities in general and the value of *erp4students* for their future job chances in particular course completion rates above 80 % in average across all national contexts and even over 90 % in Austria are a clear acknowledgement.

Even in a context like Germany, where university education generally is expected to being free of charge, students are willed to pay manageable prices for additional training offers; provided that the offers as well as the pricing are considered to be reasonable. Additionally, the learners in *erp4students* have the chance to experience substantial support from their tutors and have plenty of time to spend and experiment within the original SAP software environment – which they highly value!

For the future, we plan to implement further courses, translate existing courses to additional languages, and we aim to involve students from additional regions of the world. In order to steadily go on writing a success story, we plan to further monitor the cultural perceptions and attitudes of our learners in order to optimally support them with our course design and particularly, to prevent causing recognized cultural conflicts.

References

1. Dobischat, R., Fischell, M., Rosendahl, A.: Auswirkungen der Studienreform durch die Einführung des Bachelorabschlusses auf das Berufsausbildungssystem: Eine Problemskizze. Hans-Böckler-Stiftung, Düsseldorf (2008)
2. Columbos, L.: Gartner's ERP Market Share Update shows the Future of Cloud ERP is now (2014). http://www.forbes.com/sites/louiscolumbus/2014/05/12/gartners-erp-market-share-update-shows-the-future-of-cloud-erp-is-now/
3. Arnold, P., Kilian, L., Thillosen, A., Zimmer, G.: Handbuch E-Learning: Lehren und Lernen mit digitalen Medien, 3rd edn. Bertelsmann Verlag, Bielefeld (2013)
4. Richter, T., Adelsberger, H.H., The whole is more than the sum of its parts: on culture in education and educational culture. In: Proceedings of the 7th CSEDU, vol. 2, pp. 372–384. SCITEPRESS, Lisbon (2015)
5. Ruckriegel, K.: Glücksforschung (Happiness Research) – Erkenntnisse und Konsequenzen. Wirtschaftsphilologen Verband Bayern e. V., Mitteilungen, Nr. 193 (2010)
6. Horx, M.: Das Buch des Wandels – Wie Menschen die Zukunft gestalten. IHK Nürnberg für Mittelfranken, 450 Jahre Wirtschaftsförderung, Nürnberg (2009)
7. StudiVZ (2015). https://secure.studivz.net/Register/Step3
8. Sandanayake, T.C; Madurapperuma, A.P.: Novel approach for online learning through affect recognition. In: Proceedings of 5th International Conference on Distance Learning and Education, vol.12, pp. 72–77. IACSIT Press, Singapore (2011)
9. Müller, H.-P.: Kulturelle Gliederung der Entwicklungsländer. In: Müller, H.-P. (ed.) *Weltsystem und kulturelles Erbe*, pp. 81–137. Raimer Verlag, Berlin (1996)
10. Richter, T., Adelsberger, H.H.: On the myth of a general national culture: making specific cultural characteristics of learners in different educational contexts in Germany visible. In: CATaC 2012 Proceedings, Murdoch University, Murdoch, pp. 105–120 (2012)
11. Richter, T., McPherson, M.: Open educational resources: education for the world? Distance Education **33**(2), 201–219 (2012)
12. Buehler, E., Alayed, F., Komlodi, A., Epstein, S.: "It is magic": a global perspective on what technology means to youth. In: CATaC 2012 Proceedings, Murdoch University: Murdoch, pp. 100–104 (2012)

13. Mitra, S., Dangwal, R., Chatterjee, S., Jha, S., Bisht, R.S., Kapur, P.: Acquisition of computing literacy on shared public computers: children and the "hole in the wall". Australas. J. Educ. Technol. **21**, 407–426 (2005)
14. Davis, M.: Cultural viability of global english in creating universal meaning in technologically mediated communication. Electron. J. Commun. **15**, 2 (2005)
15. Benavot, A.: Cross-national Commonalities and Differences in the Intended Curriculum in Primary School Reading and Mathematics. UNESCO, Montreal (2011)

Embedded eLearning – on Demand Improvement of ERP Competences

Sabrina Romina Sorko[✉] and Herbert Kohlbacher

Institute of Industrial Management, FH JOANNEUM University of Applied Sciences,
Werk-VI-Strasse 46, 8605 Kapfenberg, Austria
{Sabrinaromina.Sorko,Herbert.Kohlbacher}@fh-joanneum.at

Abstract. The actual trend of Industry 4.0 affects different divisions of a company, amongst others HRM and IT. The knowledge of ERP users and their training are gaining importance. eLearning should support trainings and save costs. The following paper starts under the assumption of missing acceptance and lack of success of currently available eLearning tools. This will be checked with the help of a survey which deals with ERP systems in order to gain experience about those tools and their success. Especially thereby identified weaknesses are used to develop a more advanced eLearning-Model to improve efficiency and acceptance. A small interface, reusing existing eLearning-objects and providing materials in the right manner is presented to ERP providers, consulting companies and staff developers in companies using ERP systems.

Keywords: Embedded eLearning · ERP training · Employer competences

1 Introduction

The emerging trend industry 4.0 (I 4.0) stands for total automation in industry and postulates the future crosslinking of production and internet. Terms like Big Data, Mobile Computing or Cloud Computing find their way into the production process. This forecast leads to discussions in different fields of study around the industry [1]. Also Human Resources has to deal with wide-reaching changes.

The restructuring of jobs is a widely accepted fact, for example the human resources required for performing work directly in the production will decrease over the years, whereas higher qualified employees are in demand in the indirect areas of production [1]. In this case higher qualified means that employees must be able to communicate with different units. This implies the necessity to solve problems linking gained knowledge and be aware of consequences their actions might result in [2]. As I 4.0 stands for a mainly atomized production, besides other changes employees require IT competences in order to meet the new job requirements.

As a main interface ERP systems are widely implemented. Those systems face the challenge of supporting the key user in adapting to increased demand. Considering these arguments the research question of this paper is as follows: How can employees be

© Springer International Publishing Switzerland 2016
M. Felderer et al. (Eds.): ERP Future 2015 - Research, LNBIP 245, pp. 19–27, 2016.
DOI: 10.1007/978-3-319-32799-0_2

supported efficiently in gaining competences in ERP systems using embedded eLearning and how are the key users trained at the moment?

This paper deals with the question of how this is currently done and what actions should be taken to fulfill the drafted standards. In order to define the status quo of training methods 135 ERP providers in Austria have been surveyed. The results are compared to other research and currently required training methods. On that basis an embedded eLearning model is designed, which helps the user to train the competences while working. Therefore, different eLearning elements are integrated in the ERP system which abets learning due to the high usability and low expenditure of time.

2   Findings

Actually there are plenty of possibilities how companies train their employees in using ERP systems. Nevertheless the employer's satisfaction is quite low. Key user sense most of the ERP systems as confusing and unstructured and get discouraged while working with them. It also happens quite often, that employees feed data into the system not thinking or even realizing the impact their actions have [3].

As mentioned I 4.0 stands for an increase of employer flexibility and changing working conditions. Employees have to gain knowledge much faster in order to fulfill all requirements and be competitive in the long run. An efficient and practical method is eLearning. Because of various advantages, such as their availability, eLearning models become more and more attractive for industries. The yearly made HR-trend study by Kienbaum showed, that almost 70 percent of the companies asked[1] support digital training in order to provide flexible further education [4].

In order to answer the research question firstly it was necessary to discover how the providers of ERP systems actually train their customers. The second part of the study deals with designing an embedded eLearning model.

Competence Orientation. Within the last years further education was subjected to alteration. The so far predominant concept of input orientation was detached by output orientation and outcome orientation. The figure shows this development and how those terms are linked to each other [5] (Fig. 1).

Educational sciences realized that focusing the content of teaching is not as relevant as putting the learning outcome, the impact of training, in the center of attention. One input can lead to different outcomes depending on the individual competences the employer has [6]. In the occupational context competences, respectively the ability to make decisions responsibly, is needed in order to be a competitive employee. Relevant precondition for a successful training is the willingness of the employee. Thus motivation is the key success factor [7].

Those competences are linked to the particular field of work. When applied to key user competence orientation means that they must not only have professional skills.

---

[1] In 2015 187 HR Manager from companies in the German speaking area were surveyed by Kienbaum.

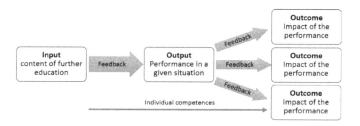

Fig. 1. From Input to Outcome

On the one hand employees have to use the ERP system responsibly. On the one hand operator safety must be given, as well as awareness of what consequences their own actions cause in other areas of the company. To train these competences ERP providers offer several methods of training.

2.1 Key User Training – Status Quo

To determine how ERP system providers train their key users an online questionnaire was sent to 135 companies in Austria. After an answering period of five weeks, 38 questionnaire were answered. This equates to a return rate of nearly 30 %. The aim of the study was to define what training methods are currently offered, what experiences they made and what new training methods will be implemented within the next years. Those results are compared with the status quo in further education.

Key user Training Status Quo. The analysis shows, that more than 97 % of the ERP provider offer different types of training for their key user. Also more than 80 % believe that ERP training is very important in order to work efficiently and successfully. This data underlines the high significance of accompanying software training. For that reason providing companies tend to enhance their customer service program continuously.

The range of aiding methods those companies offer is wide. Within the study the most established training methods are named. Furthermore, the proband can expand upon the pre-existing list (Fig. 2).

In comparison the figure shows the actual offered training methods as well as those deemed especially successful. It reveals that in-house training is not only the most offered tool but it also is highly demanded by the customers. Secondly, online support is referred to by ERP providers which means for example supporting websites or support via email. Uncommon but at least referenced by every fourth company is the printed handbook. When comparing those numbers with what can be seen as best practice, there are some substantial differences. Aside from in-house training the surveyed companies deemed none of the methods as especially successful regarding the customer feedback. The largest difference is found for online support. Although only 20 % name those methods as having good feedback by the costumers, nearly 70 % of the ERP provider offer such tools. The situation of handbooks is also remarkable. Online handbooks are used by 50 % of the providers, although only 16 % regard them as especially successful

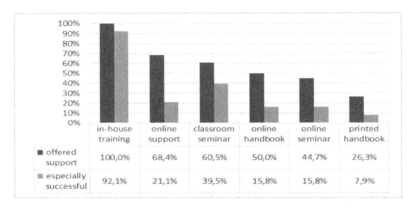

Fig. 2. Training methods offered by ERP providers versus especially successful methods

and the same situation is given for printed ones. It is also conspicuous, that all online training methods are not very popular.

Those results lead to two main questions:

- Why do ERP providers offer online training methods?
- Why are online methods not especially preferred by the customers?

In order to answer this questions the participants were asked why some methods are more successful than others. Summing up the customers and providers needs, following requirements can be deduced (Fig. 3).

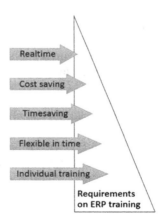

Fig. 3. Requirements on ERP training

ERP supporting methods should cover three main aspects. Training tools have to conserve resources in order to ensure high efficiency. Thereby not only low personnel costs and travel expenses can be realized but also saving of time. Related to this there is the need of individuality. As every customer has needs based on their individual processes also training methods should be customized. The optimal ERP supporting system has to be a flexible model developed also with the customers. Considering that, an embedded eLearning model will be introduced.

2.2 Embedded eLearning

A lot of eLearning tools for ERP systems already exist but they are not embedded. The figure below points out the main differences between classroom learning, traditional eLearning and embedded eLearning (Fig. 4).

		classroom	eLearning	embedded eLearning
costs	course fee	usual	possible	possible on demand
	travel costs	yes	none	none
	absence	several days	hours	on demand
time	course time	fix	intended duration	individual, on demand
	travel time	depends on location of the training	none	none
technical	learning material	books	multimedial	multimedial, system-integrated
	systems	ERP	eLearning-plattform, ERP	eLearning-plattform, ERP
challenge		content be left behind after course	managing (ir)relevant content	maintenance

Fig. 4. Classroom learning, eLearning and embedded eLearning in comparison

While eLearning helps to reduce costs by avoiding travel time of employees, embedded eLearning improves the efficiency by providing the required information on demand. The user decides on the scope of content and kind of material depending of his preferences and learning type. Mobile devices support the way to learn anywhere and anytime and encourage the motivation. The sum of these features shall lead to more efficiency and works against loss and forgetting.

Embedded eLearning Model. On the basis of actual literature the possibility of embedding innovative eLearning elements in an ERP system, in this context SAP, was identified. Whereat each integration is linked to existing eLearning approaches and analyzed regarding its integration possibility.

The developed model consists of two main parts. First the integration of an eLearning course linked directly to several applications within the system. Second several simulations in order to increase the employees' awareness of their actions.

Integrated eLearning Course. On the one hand an eLearning platform has to be integrated in the system. In this section learning material such as handbooks, tutorials, presentations or videos for different sections of the ERP system are available. Those materials are linked directly to the equivalent application in the system.

Real Time Embedded eLearning Elements. On the other hand every input box should be provided with a drop down icon where the key user can choose between different types of support. The drop down menu offers five different supporting tools.

- Description
- Value-list
- Simulation
- Comparison
- eLearning course

The first option *description* contains the meaning and purpose of the corresponding field. In SAP this option is known as Field Help and will displayed after pressing the F1 Key. When integrated directly into the system a key user who does not know about the F1 support can get information more easily. The *value-list* is also already existent and should be preserved. It overviews the given input variants for the particular field and is known as input help (F4) in SAP. The *simulation* function supports the holistic thinking of the employees. When entering data into a specific input box, the simulation shows how this current action would influence different other parts of the company. When using this tool, the key user gets a better idea on the impact of their work which occurs in a responsibility increase. Similar to the simulation is the *comparison* that allows to compare values with similar data respectively the current master data object with further objects and the entered values there. This helps the user to estimate the accuracy of information and to get a better understanding in validity. The fifth option is linked to the *eLearning* area of the ERP system. In this part all learning tools that support the user in gaining ERP competences are prepared. The organization should be verified to the individual needs of the company. For all materials it is important that they open in a separate pop up so that the key user keeps the process step they are currently working on. In addition when moving the cursor over the input box the key user is provided with a brief explanation of the application.

3   Discussion

When looking at future development, one third of the surveyed ERP providers named eLearning as a training method they tend to implement within the next years. This confirms the high priority ERP developers should give to those supporting systems. But, as drafted, general eLearning is not the ideal solution. In fact an embedded eLearning system is needed in order to fulfill the customer respectively key user needs. Therefore, extensions in the existing ERP systems are necessary.

Interface Between ERP and eLearning. The opportunity to reuse learning materials, like videos, tutorials or quizzes, is one key requirement of the embedded eLearning model. These objects should be displayed in overlapping, moveable and resizable frames over the ERP client. Open standards like HTML5 enable the integration of learning material. The solution providers has to extend their client software to be able to invoke the communication dialogue as shown in the model. Similar to tool tips, developers may call the help dialog automatically after a certain time of inactivity. Also, time of inactivity or a randomizer can be used to start a short quiz in order to improve knowledge by testing and refreshing information.

The trend to modern architecture predicated on web-based frontends promotes the chance to extent such clients to integrate eLearning content. To be able to address the right learning objects, a unique identifier is necessary. The development of such identifiers has to be standardized in order to reuse learning objects.

Strengths and Potentials. Looking at the SWOT analysis below, that high potentials are accompanied by comparatively less risks and weaknesses (Fig. 5).

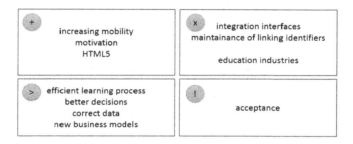

Fig. 5. SWOT analysis of embedded eLearning

Increasing mobility and the spread of smartphones promotes the implementation of (embedded) eLearning systems, just like the actual trend to HTML5/UI5-based clients on the technical side. Efforts to develop the interface, organize identifiers, maintain and update learning materials must be made. Thus training organization have to adopt their business process and/or model – changing from classroom courses to eLearning platforms. Anyway default risks among a lack of acceptance are existing.

4   Conclusion

Due to the outlined conditions, flexible and motivating learning environments have to be designed in order to support ERP key users adequately. A direct integration into the ERP system also simplifies the availability of learning elements. The immediate accessibility results in a reduction of training barriers. Moreover occurring uncertainties can be compensated contemporary which causes an increase of motivation. Therefore, embedded eLearning models turn out to be well suited because of their permanent and real time availability as well as their flexibility (Fig. 6).

The comparison of the drafted requirements on ERP training systems with the advantages of embedded eLearning models can provide indicates that there is still one component which has to be discussed. The detailed procedure of implementing such an interface has to be designed by developers of different ERP system providers and strongly depends on the used technologies, but should address a broad standard.

Fig. 6. Status quo of ERP training

Current and Comparable Developments. SAP is one of the leading ERP developers regarding those new requirements. They actually provide so called guided procedures in SAP S/4 on HANA, which are a good example of integration learning objects and ERP via HTML5 in parallel.[2] The difference to embedded eLearning are the trigger and the provided content.

In conclusion it can be stated, that actually there is a need for flexible, resource saving and individual ERP training methods that cannot be fully satisfied at the moment. Nevertheless some ERP developers like SAP are continuously working on new web solutions. However, wide interventions in the system will be necessary to meet the demands of the key user. In regards to this, embedded eLearning represents an innovative training model.

References

1. Spath, D., Ganschar, O., Gerlach, S., Hämmerle, M., Krause, T., Schlund, S.: Produktionsarbeit der Zukunft – Industrie 4.0, Studie Fraunhofer-Institut für Arbeitswirtschaft und Organisation, Stuttgart (2013)
2. Botthof, A., Hartmann, E.A.: Zukunft der Arbeit in Industrie 4.0. Springer Vieweg, Berlin (2015)
3. Sontow K., Treutlein P., Sontow R.: ERP in der Praxis - Anwenderzufriedenheit, Nutzen & Perspektiven, Trovarit (2014)
4. Kienbaum: Ergebnisbericht HR-Trendstudie (2015). http://www.kienbaum.at/Portaldata/1/Resources/downloads/brochures/Kienbaum_HR-Trendstudie_FINAL.pdf

---

[2] Under https://go.sap.com/germany/cmp/oth/crm-s4hana/index.html, SAP provides a free trial to SAP S/4HANA.

5. Slepcevic-Zach, P., Tafner, G.: Input-Output-Outcome: Alle reden von Kompetenzorientierung, aber meinen alle dasselbe? Versuch einer Kategorisierung. In: Paechter, M., Stock, M., Schmölzer-Eibinger, S., Slepcevic-Zach, P., Weirer, W. (Hrsg) Handbuch Kompetenzorientierter Unterricht, S. 27–41. Beltz-Verlag, Weinheim (2012)
6. Storz, P.: Wandel von Anforderungen in beruflicher Arbeit – Konsequenzen für berufliche Aus- und Fortbildung. In: Wiesner, G., Wolter, A. (Hrsg) Die lernende Gesellschaft, S. 79–95. Juventa Verlag, Weinheim (2005)
7. Jana-Tröller, M.: Arbeitsübergreifende Kompetenzen älterer Arbeitnehmer. Eine qualitative Studie in einem Telekommunikationsunternehmen, Verlag für Sozialwissenschaften, Wiesbaden (2009)

Business Process Models

Business Process Model Semantics in BPMN

Peter Bollen[✉]

School of Business and Economics, Maastricht University, Maastricht, The Netherlands
p.bollen@maastrichtuniversity.nl

Abstract. In this article we will provide an overview of Business Process Modeling notations as they have evolved over the past 50 years within the field of information systems. The emphasis in this article will be on the contemporary OMG standard for Business Process Modeling Notations: BPMN. We will analyze the BPMN notation on the ontological, the organizational and the aggregation perspectives. The suitability of the BPMN as a business process modeling notation within model-driven architectures will be discussed.

Keywords: BPMN · Business process modeling · Business process management · Business process model semantics

1 Introduction

In the nineteen-fifties the first large-scale 'administrative' computer applications came into use in organizations. The functionality of these electronic data processing (EDP) systems was an exact copy of the manual procedures that until then had been applied by a large number of clerks in these corporations. The focus was on transaction processing applications. The process perspective for these applications consisted of routine tasks descriptions with a limited scope. Information Systems (IS) were primarily used to replace clerical staff by machines, which resulted in an enhanced operational transaction efficiency [1]. The coding of these applications was completed by IS professionals leaving the end users in many cases aside [1].

The 'waterfall-based' IS development methodologies from the 1960's and 1970's were very rigid, and in many projects this lead to significant cost overruns and delayed delivery times. By the time an information systems project was finished, the initial organizational requirements had already been changed. In many cases, however, the information systems development methodologies had not been able to capture the initial requirements in the right way in the first place. In the 1960's a distinction was made between the roles of 'user' and 'programmer', in this era the role of analyst and developer coincided: "In the pre-methodology era [prior to 1970], systems developers used a variety of techniques to help them develop computer-based information systems….They [techniques] were typically passed on to other systems developers, often by word of mouth. These rules or techniques were typically not codified and sometimes not written down…..Systems development was considered a technical process to be undertaken by technical people. In this era, systems development was all art and no science." [2].

© Springer International Publishing Switzerland 2016
M. Felderer et al. (Eds.): ERP Future 2015 - Research, LNBIP 245, pp. 31–45, 2016.
DOI: 10.1007/978-3-319-32799-0_3

In the 1970's a clear separation started to take place between the functional requirements of an information systems application (the *what* question) and the way in which these functional requirements were coded in a specific implementation technology [3] (the *how* question). The distinctive roles of *information analyst* and *systems developer* were created. Information Systems Development Methodologies were aimed at the creation of 'tailor-made' information systems in which the specific needs of the users in the organization was the starting point.

When the type of information systems applications that were needed in organizations became more strategic (e.g. airline reservation systems, enterprise resource planning (ERP)) the developers attitude was by and large still the same. Information systems that were the result of applying the craftsmanship of the fifties and sixties, proved to be too costly to develop, often not delivered on time and failed to comply to the specified functionality.

The information systems development market place, however, changed in the early nineties of the last century when the *product software*-suppliers, e.g. MFG/PRO, IFS, SAP, BAAN, Marshal, Peoplesoft [4] started to sell their enterprise solutions on the waves of the Business Process Reengineering (BPR) sea [5, 6]. These product software solutions promised to solve many problems that characterized the 'tailor-made' information systems projects. The implementation of these ERP systems in a company in most cases implied that (at least some of) the business processes had to be reengineered [7] or redesigned [8, 9] to fit the 'reference-model(s)' that underly(ies) the ERP package. In addition ERP implementations might require changes in the organizational structure, reports and procedures [10]. Process redesign turned out to be feasible for standard application functionality, for example, accounting, payroll, human resource management and inventory control.

In the ERP era (1990 and onwards) the roles of the user (or domain expert), analyst and developer were becoming more iterative instead of the linear 'waterfall-based' sequence in which those roles were performed in the decades before. Because the implementation of ERP-systems usually is linked to business process redesign or a business process reengineering exercise, the role of the user or domain expert becomes more complex. In cooperation with the ERP-analyst the domain expert has to evaluate a number of proposed ways of working that can potentially be supported by the ERP software [11]. However, company-specific, functionality remained a problem in the first generation ERP-solutions. The second generation ERP-solutions, however, tried to redefine the concept of company-specific functionality by developing 'standardized' software solutions for specific 'branches', for example, health-care, utilities, retail, e-commerce and so forth. The development of the additional functionality in these second generation ERP systems, implied, in many cases, additional reengineering efforts on these branche-specific domains before an implementation could take place. In spite of the availability of these second generation ERP solutions, many companies needed customized modules and interfaces that allowed them to support the specific parts of their business [12]. Soffer et al. [12] discuss in the context of ERP requirement-driven alignment the necessity of the construction of a modeling language that can model the entire scope of ERP options.

In this article we will analyze the semantics of the *Business Process Modeling Notation* (BPMN). BPMN is an OMG standard that is inspired by earlier (business) process modeling notations, e.g. *flowcharts*, *data flow diagrams* (DFD's) [13], *state-transition diagrams* (STD's) [14] and notations embedded in more comprehensive modeling approaches or methods, e.g. IDEF (especially IDEF$_0$ *functional models* and IDEF$_3$ *process flow diagrams* and *object state transition networks*) [15, 16], ARIS (especially *EPC* diagrams) [17] and UML (especially *activity diagrams* and *state chart* diagrams) [18, 19].

1.1 Overview and Structure of Article

The underlying objectives for the development of BPMN were to create a business process modeling notation that firstly allows organizational stake-holders to communicate using a 'standardized' business process modeling language and secondly allow for an easy model-driven implementation [20]. This 'double' objective sets BPMN apart from earlier notations and methods. This means that in the discussion on BPMN in this article, we will first zoom in on those modeling constructs that are necessary for communicating the 'essence' of business process models to all possible stakeholders. In Sect. 2 an overview of business process modeling notations within the field of information systems development will be given. In Sect. 3 we will introduce the group of essential modeling constructs in BPMN. In Sect. 4 we will give an ontology for the BPMN modeling constructs to be considered relevant in this article. In Sect. 5 we will discuss some of the advanced modeling BPMN concepts that can be used to capture additional semantics that can be exploited whenever IT-solutions have to be developed to support organizational business processes, for example, workflow-management application or a web-based retail system. In Sect. 6 we will discuss some of the decomposition properties of the BPMN. Finally, in Sect. 7 conclusions will be given.

2 Overview of Modeling Methods and Notations for Business Processes

In the 1960's and 1970's the development of large company information systems was taking off. A large emphasis was placed on the 'automation' of manual administrative processes. For the purpose of 'automating' or 'mechanizing' these routine administrative processes, a number of IS methodologies were developed. One of the most dominant modeling schools was the 'structured analysis and design' approach [21–23]. In this modeling school the emphasis was on 'processes' and the 'data-flow' between processes. The data aspects were considered to be less important. In the 1970's more comprehensive approaches that would focus on change processes as well were developed (e.g., [24]). In the late 1970's and in the 1980's, methodologies for developing (business) information systems started to put more emphasis on the data-aspects of the information system. Approaches like (Extended) Entity-Relationship modeling (E)E-R [25, 26], NIAM [27, 28] and Infomod [29] emerged that put the emphasis on data-aspect of the IS development process. In the late eighties and early nineties the insights from object-oriented programming, provided the foundation for a number of object-oriented IS development approaches, i.e. OMT [30] and OOSE [31]. In 1997 the combined development of three of these methodologies culminated in the design of a new 'object-oriented' modeling approach for IS development (among other application areas): the Unified Modeling Language (UML) [18, 19]. This language later became an OMG (Object Management Group) standard.

In the ERP era a number of business process modeling approaches were developed. An approach that was used in SAP documentation and by SAP consultancy firms was ARIS [17, 32].

In the first decade of the 21st century the management of business processes once again became a high priority on the strategic agenda of a large number of organizations. Business Process Management became a top priority because a large number of organizations needed to improve their cost-effectiveness by considering to off-shore 'knowledge-intensive' processes to lower wage destinations, for example India, Malaysia and the Phillipines. Well-defined measurable processes that are self-contained are the primary candidates to offshore [33]. This renewed interest for knowledge-intensive business processes paved the way for an industry consortium (the business process management initiative) to develop a business process modeling notation which can be used by organizations to capture, document and to subsequently redesign specific business processes thereby improving their structural metrics [34]. The name of the OMG standard that was developed by the Business Process Management Perspective is the *Business Process Model and Notation* (BPMN) (see for the documentation of version 1.1. [35]). This standard defines the modeling constructs for creating business process models.

BPMN was developed with the primary goal of providing a notation that would be readily understandable by all business users, from business analysts to technical developers that will have to implement the technology [20, p. 1] and the need to translate 'original' business process models into 'execution' models.

3   The Essential Modeling Constructs in the BPMN Standard for Business Process Models

The basic BPMN concepts can be classified into *flow objects*, *connectors* and *artifacts* [20]. In Fig. 1 we have given the graphical representations of the most important BPMN modeling constructs.

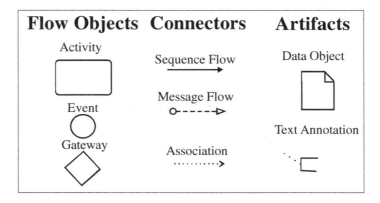

Fig. 1. Diagrammatic representation of most important BPMN modeling concepts

3.1   Flow Objects in BPMN

The essential modeling concepts in the BPMN that capture the essence of the business processes within an organization are the Flow objects. The flow objects in BPMN consists of *activities*, *events* and gateways. 'An *activity* is a generic term for work that a company performs. The types of activities that are a part of a process model are: *process, sub-process* and *task* [35]. An activity is work that is performed within a business process. A *task* is an atomic activity that can not be broken down to (a) finer level of activity [20]. A *sub-process* is a non-atomic or compound activity that can be broken down into a set of sub-activities [20].

'An *event* is something that happens during the course of a business process' [34].

'A *gateway* is used to control the divergence and convergence of sequence flow' [35]. Gateways in BPMN are used to control the sequence flow in terms of convergence and divergence and a gateway has a number of attributes.

3.2   Connectors in BPMN

The next group of modeling elements in BPMN are the connectors. Their main function is to connect the flow objects in a number of ways. There are basically three types of connectors in BPMN: *sequence flow, message flow* and an *association.*

A *sequence flow* depicts the order in which the connected activities are performed: 'A sequence flow is used to show the order that activities will be performed in a process' [35].

A *message flow* shows a flow of messages between two objects. An association is used to relate *artifacts* with *flow objects* and is mainly used to show the (data) *inputs* and (data) *outputs* of *activities.*

'An *association* is used to associate information flow with flow objects' [35]. '*data objects* are considered artifacts because they do not have any direct effect on the sequence flow or message flow of the process, but they do provide information about what activities required to be performed and/or what they produce' [35].

3.3   Artifacts in BPMN

In addition to the groups of flow object and the group of connectors, BPMN has a group of modeling concepts that are considered to be of less importance to capture the essence of business models. This group of modeling concepts is called artifacts in BPMN. A *data object* is one of the two artifact types that are currently defined in the BPMN standard [35]. The 'incorporation' or 'leaving-out' of data-objects in a process model, is a way for some modelers to leave out 'clutter' [35]. The data object is a very significant modeling concept in BPMN because it is the primary modeling construct [36] that will allow a business process modeler to 'connect' the BPMN model to the conceptual schema that underlies the database of the organization.

A *text annotation* can be used to provide comment on the BPMN modeling element to which it is connected.

4 A BPMN Ontology

In line with the definition of Gruber [37] and the work of McCarthy [38] we define an ontology as a semantic definition of a field's objects, concepts and other entitities and the relationships among them. Gailly et al. [39] give an overview of ontology classification schemes and frameworks for ontology applications. In this section we will specify the domain ontology for BPMN that has an internal structure that consists of a list of semantic definitions (terms/glossary) of the modeling concepts and the relations between concepts. In Table 1 a small excerpt of the list of semantic definitions is provided for the essential BPMN modeling constructs.

Table 1. Excerpt of list of semantic definitions for the main model elements BPMN standard.

Concept	Definition
Activity	An activity is work that is performed within a business
Process	A Process is any [Activity] performed within or across companies or organization
Process name	A name that designates a specific [Process] among the union of [Process]es

In as far as the relationships between the concepts are concerned we will give a small sample of the relationships between the objects and concepts from the BPMN ontology.

The **Black-Box Pool** has an outgoing **MessageFlow** to the **Task** that is defined within a **SubProcess.**

This is just one example of dozens of relationships that (potentially) exist between the BPMN model elements. These relationships can also be graphically modeled by using for example an E-R notational convention [25] as is exemplified in Fig. 2.

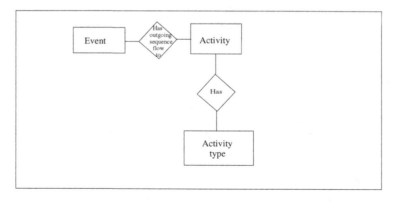

Fig. 2. E-R model excerpt for BPMN domain relationship ontology

4.1 An Example Application of the Essential BPMN Modeling Constructs

In Fig. 3 we have given an example BPMN diagram that is loosely based upon the example that was given in Carnaghan [40]. In this example we will apply the BPMN modeling concepts of Fig. 1 in a straightforward way. The process that is modeled here is the business process *Goods Return*. For now we have distinguished two activities within the process *Goods return*: *Inspect returned goods* and *Give return authorization*.

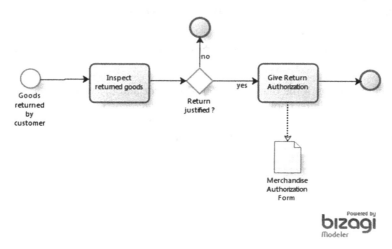

Fig. 3. Example BPMN model using the essential BPMN modeling concepts

Furthermore, we have a start event *Goods returned by customer* and we have two end events that will end this process. Furthermore we find one gateway: *Return justified*. If the gateway condition ('return satisfied?') is not true, the sequence flow will lead to an end event and the process will terminate. In case the condition is fulfilled the activity *Give Return Authorization* can take place. This activity will create an instance of a *Merchandise authorization form*. After this activity has taken place the process will end. In the BPMN diagram of Fig. 3 we also find 5 sequence flows and one association between the activity *Give return authorization* and the data object *Merchandise Authorization form*.

5 Additional Modeling Constructs in the BPMN Standard for Business Process Models

For a number of sub-types of BPMN modeling concepts additional attributes are defined. For example for the *event* modeling concept we have as an attribute the event type, that must either have the value: *start, end* or *intermediate*.

In addition to the modeling constructs that were depicted in Fig. 1 and applied in the example of Fig. 3, BPMN has a modeling construct that can be used to demarcate the borders of a process (or set of processes) from an (functional) organizational structure point of view: the swimlane. In BPMN two types of *swimlane* constructs can be used: *pools* and *lanes*. The *pool* concept allows modelers to specify message flows between two (or more) separate business entities. The *lane* construct can be used to show how certain activities are associated with a specific company function [20, pp. 4–5]. A distinction is made into *white box* and *black box* pools [36]. A *white box* pool is a pool that reveals the underlying structure at least in terms of top-layer *flow-objects* and *connectors*. A black box pool can serve as a sender or receiver of message flows but it can not reveal the underlying *flow-objects* and *connectors*.

5.1   An Example Application of the Essential and Additional BPMN Modeling Constructs

In the example of Fig. 4 the black box pool *Customer* and the white-box pool *Goods return* are given. The latter pool is divided into two *swimlanes*. The division of the model elements into these swimlanes is based upon the organizational function (or department) that is involved. Most of the elements in the 'swimlane free' diagram in Fig. 3 have been

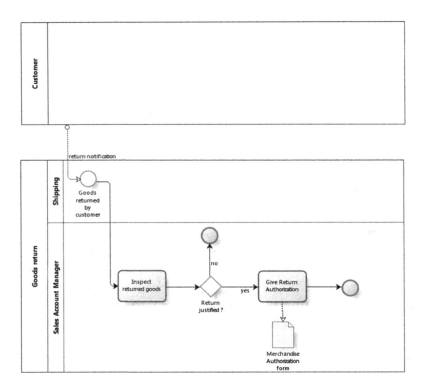

Fig. 4. Example BPMN model using the essential and additional BPMN modeling concepts

placed differently in the vertical dimension to relate them to an organizational function or 'actor' that is responsible for the execution of the activity. The only 'real' difference between the diagrams in Figs. 3 and 4 is the message flow *return notification* that is send by the black-box pool 'Customer' and which initiates the former start event of the process: *goods returned by customer.*

BPMN does not only have 'graphical' modeling concepts, it also contains a large number of attributes that can be attached to the graphical modeling concepts and that can be assigned values for each instance of a concept in a process model. As an example of how we can use the process attributes to capture additional the semantics of a business activity we will show how the description of these semantics can reference elements from an (integrated) data model or conceptual schema. In Fig. 5 we have given an excerpt of a (part of) an enterprise-wide conceptual schema [38] using Chen's Entity-Relationship (E-R) notation [25]. The elements from this conceptual data schema are referenced in the semantic description of the activity: give return authorization in the BPMN process model in Figs. 3 and 4.

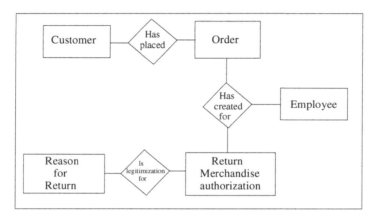

Fig. 5. Relevant excerpt from enterprise-wide conceptual schema for business activity *give return authorization*

We can now instantiate the values for some of the attributes for the BPMN modeling concept activity type: *Give return authorization.* This activity can be a manual activity (user task) or an automated activity (service task). Let's assume for now that the activity *give return authorization* is a user task. The outcome of such an activity in most if not all cases will consists of (structured) information and in many cases (structured) information will be used as input to a user task. Let's assume that in our process example *Goods return* the actor that is responsible for 'acting' in the activity needs first information about which customer has placed the order that is now offered as return merchandise, furthermore he needs to know the reason for return. So in order to make a decision whether to authorize the merchandise return or not, the 'actor' of the *give return authorization* activity (within the *return goods process*) will use instances of the relationships **has placed** and **is legitimization for**. The result of this activity will be an instance of the relationship **has created for** in case a return authorization is granted. We can link the specification of an activity, therefore to the content of the conceptual data schema of the integrated enterprise by listing the relationships as values for the activity attributes (see Table 2).

Table 2. Attribute values for user activity: return merchandise authorization

Attributes	Prop/attribute	Value
Activity type		Task: return merchandise authorization
Input set	artifactInput	Relationships: **has placed** and **is legitimization for**
Output set	artifactOutput	Relationship: **has created for**

Under the assumption that the activity/task *Return merchandise authorization* is a service task, it must be possible to specify a set of business rules that can be implemented in a IT application. Hence, the suitability of BPMN to be a notation that contains sufficient modeling constructs in order to be used within a Model-Driven architecture (MDA) We can specify th(i)e(se) business rule(s) as values of the IOrules attribute of a BPMN activity (see Table 3).

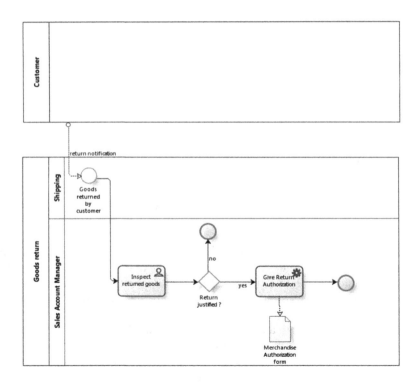

Fig. 6. Example BPMN model using activity/task typing

Table 3. Attribute values for service activity: return merchandise authorization

Attributes	Prop/attribute	Value
Activity type		Task: return merchandise organization
Input set	artifactInput	Relationships: **has placed** and **is legitimization for**
Output set	artifactOutput	Relationship: **has created for**
IOrules		IF **is legitimization for. reason for return** = 'damaged goods' THEN create **return merchandize.authorization**

In Fig. 6 we have shown the BPMN process model from Fig. 4, in which we have now explicitly typed each activity/task as either a *user task* or a *service task* by attaching the appropriate symbol from the BPMN standard. This distinction within activities can only be created whenever an activity is a task. This means that such a task-activity: '… has no internal subparts defined by the model.' [36] and therefore is not further decomposable.

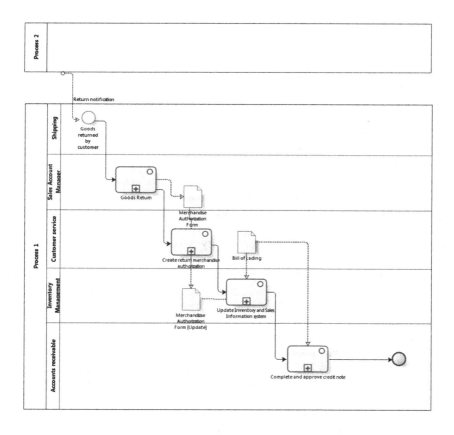

Fig. 7. Overview BPMN model using expandable sub-processes

6   Collapsed and Expanded Processes

A process modeling property that been featured in many 'earlier' process modeling notations like *DFD*'s, *ISACA-schemes, IDEF functional schemas* is stepwise refinement or decomposition and its inverse. In BPMN this feature is called (hierarchical) expansion [36] and its inverse is called collapsing. This means that in terms of BPMN business process diagrams we might have a set of different business process models in which subsets of process models will refer to higher levels of expansion. The concept of collapsing/expanding in essence allows stakeholders to create 'overview' diagrams on every desired level of granularity. In the BPMN standard there is a modeling construct that we can assign to an activity to mark such an activity as 'further decomposable' or as 'non-decomposable'. In the latter case we will call the activity a *task*. In Fig. 7 we have given an overview process diagram in which the process *goods return* is collapsed as a 'higher level' sub-process. To denote that this sub-process can be expanded, BPMN attaches the '+' symbol on the activity symbol.

7   Conclusion

The application of the BPMN as a notation for business process models does not guarantee the alignment of conceptual documents in the data-perspective, e.g. relational models, (E)E-R diagrams, UML class diagrams, data repositories with the process models. The use of the data-object in BPMN does not enforce the compliance to an integrated conceptual data model of a business organization (when such a model is available). To define this 'misalignment' from a different point-of-view, we can say that, in a fully process-oriented approach the creation of BPMN models does not enforce the creation of a relevant increment of the integrated conceptual data schema.

BPMN allows business process analysts to create pools and swimlanes that exemplify the link between events, processes, tasks, activities, sequence-flows, message-flows, gateways, data-objects and the organizational function, actor or department that is responsible for such an event, task, or activity. When it comes to assigning organizational responsibilities for data-objects things become slightly more complex, because the actual content of a data-object might consists of multiple entity attributes and/or multiple relationships between entities or multiple UML class (attributes) and/or relationships. In general, it is possible that different organizational actors/functions will be responsible for different data elements within one data-object.

Furthermore, without an actual organizational commitment to a process-based organization in which 'process-owners' will be formally assigned responsibilities in an organization for *(sub)-processes, activities, tasks* and *data-objects*, the application of any business process modeling notation by itself will not lead to the required process improvements.

BPMN provides modeling facilities that support expansion. On the other hand BPMN does not enforce modelers to expand their process models until all activities are *tasks*, i.e. activities that are no longer decomposable. This means that is possible that when a set of business process models is used to define a new or 'to-be' organizational process, fundamental data requirements will be overlooked. All information that is required within a non-expanded non-atomic activity, therefore will not be captured in a conceptual business process model, and therefore compliance to an enterprise-wide (conceptual) data model or repository can not be enforced at all times.

When we consider the aggregation levels in modeling business processes two main modeling approaches can be considered. The first modeling approach is the 'top-down' approach in which organizational actors define an overview process model. The (sub)-processes that are defined on this overview-level can be further decomposed (or expanded) into process models that show a finer level of detail. The sub-processes on any level might already be defined on a task-level, i.e. non-further decomposable activities or tasks. This means that in terms of the BPMN, the application of a 'top-down' process modeling approach might lead to rework because the exact value for the process-type (attribute) can only be established if the next-lower process model level has been created.

The second modeling approach for creating multiple levels of business process models is the 'bottom-up approach'. The practical limitations of this approach are caused by the fact that without a clear modeling methodology or procedure: '...necessary in designing the sequence of forming and elaborating components of a target process.' [40], it is very cumbersome to start defining process activities that are exactly on the lowest level of decomposition, i.e. non-further decomposable tasks.

In this article we have analyzed the BPMN as the contemporary member of the family of (business) process modeling notations. We first introduced the essential BPMN modeling concepts: *flow objects* and *sequence flows* that can be used to capture the essence of the conceptual business process models. These modeling constructs, have been around in most if not all predecessor notations for business process modeling, e.g. flowcharts, data flow diagrams and activity diagrams. Furthermore, we have discussed the (non-graphical) attributes that are defined for the core BPMN modeling elements. These non-graphical attributes allow us to capture completely and precisely the remaining formal properties of the conceptual models in the process perspective of a subject-area.

References

1. Jan, T.-S., Tsai, F.-L.: A systems view of the evolution in information systems development. Syst. Res. Behav. Sci. **19**, 61–75 (2002)
2. Hirschheim, R., Klein, H.: Paradigmatic influence on IS development methodology: evolution and conceptual advances. In: Yovits, M. (ed.) Advances in Computers. Jai Press, London (1992)
3. Tsichritzis, D., Klug, A.: The ANSI/X3/SPARC DBMS framework. Inform. Syst. **3**, 173–191 (1978)
4. Siriginidi, S.: Enterprise resource planning in reengineering business. Bus. Proc. Manag. **6**(5), 376–391 (2000)
5. Davenport, T., Short, J.: The new industrial engineering: information technology and business process redesign. Sloan Management Review (summer): 11–27 (1990)
6. Hammer, M.: Reengineering work: don't automate, obliterate. Harvard Business Review **68**, 104–112 (1990)

7. Skok, W., Legge, M.: Evaluating enterprise resource planning (ERP) systems using an interpretive approach. Knowl. Process Manage. **9**(2), 72–82 (2002)
8. Davenport, T.: Putting the enterprise into the enterprise system. Harvard Bus. Rev. **76**(4), 121–131 (1998)
9. Rolland, C., Prakash, N.: Bridging the gap between organisational needs and ERP functionality. Requir. Eng. **5**, 180–193 (2000)
10. Dillard, J.F., Ruchala, L., et al.: Enterprise resource planning systems: A physical manifestation of administrative evil. Int. J. Account. Inform. Syst. **6**, 107–127 (2005)
11. Soffer, P., Golany, B., et al.: Modelling off-the-shelf information systems requirements: an ontological approach. Requir. Eng. **6**, 183–199 (2001)
12. Soffer, P., Golany, B., et al.: ERP modeling: a comprehensive approach. Inform. Syst. **28**(6), 18 (2003)
13. Stevens, W.P., Myers, G.J., et al.: Structured design. IBM Syst. J. **13**(2), 115–139 (1974)
14. Parnas, D.L.: On the use of transition diagrams in the design of a user interface for an interactive computer system. ACM 1969, Proceedings of the 1969 24th International Conference. ACM, New-York (1969)
15. Bravoco, R., Yadav, S.: A methodology to model the functional structure of an organization. Comput. Ind. **6**, 345–361 (1985)
16. Kusiak, A., Larson, T.N., et al.: Reengineering of design and manufacturing processes. Comput. Ind. Eng. **26**(3), 521–536 (1994)
17. Scheer, A.: ARIS Business Process Modeling, 2nd edn. Springer, Berlin (1999)
18. Rumbaugh, J., Jacobson, I., et al.: The Unified Modeling Langauge Reference Manual. Addison-Wesley, Boston (1999)
19. Booch, G., Rumbaugh, J., et al.: Unified Modeling Language User Guide. Addison-Wesley Professional, Boston (2005)
20. White, S.A.: Introduction to BPMN. On demand business (2006)
21. Yourdon, E., Constantine, L.: Structured Design: Fundamentals of a Discipline. Yourdon-Press, Upper Saddle River (1979)
22. Connor, M.: Structured Analysis and Design Technique. Waltham (1980)
23. Yourdon, E.: Modern Structured Analysis. Prentice-Hall, Englewood Cliffs (1988)
24. Lundeberg, M., Goldkuhl, G., et al.: A systematic approach to information systems development. Inform. Syst. **4**(1–12), 93–118 (1979)
25. Chen, P.: The entity-relationship model: toward a unified view. ACM Trans. Database Syst. **1**(1), 9–36 (1976)
26. Teorey, T., Yang, D., et al.: A logical design methodology for relational databases using the extended E-R model. ACM Comput. Surv. **18**(2), 197–222 (1986)
27. Verheijen, G., van Bekkum, J.: NIAM: An Information Analysis method. In: IFIP TC-8 CRIS-I Conference, North-Holland, Amsterdam (1982)
28. Wintraecken, J.: The NIAM Information Analysis Method: Theory and Practice. Springer, New York (1990)
29. Jardine, D.A., van Griethuysen, J.J.: Specification of information systems operations in INFOMOD. Data Knowl. Eng. **2**(3), 177–190 (1987)
30. Rumbaugh, J.: OMT Insights: Perspective on Modeling from the Journal of Object Oriented Programming. Cambridge University Press, Cambridge (1997)
31. Jacobson, I.: Object-oriented Software Engineering: A Use CASE Approach. Addison Wesley, New York (1992)
32. Scheer, A.: Business Process Engineering: reference models for industrial enterprises. Springer, Berlin (1998)

33. Tas, J., Sunder, S.: Financial Services: business process outsourcing. Commun. ACM **47**(5), 50–52 (2004)
34. Balasubramanian, S., Gupta, M.: Structural metrics for goal based business process design and evaluation. Bus. Process Manage. J. **11**(6), 1463–7154 (2005)
35. OMG: Business Process Model and Notation (BPMN) Version 2.0, OMG (2010)
36. Silver, B.: BPMN Method & Style. Aptos, Cody-Cassidy Press (2009)
37. Gruber, T.: A translation approach to portable ontologies. Knowl. Acquis. **5**(2), 199–220 (1993)
38. McCarthy, W.E.: The REA accounting model: a generalized framework for accounting systems in a shared data environment. Account. Rev. **57**(3), 554–578 (1982)
39. Gailly, F., Laurier, W., et al.: Positioning and formalizing the REA enterprise ontology. J. Inform. Syst. **22**(2), 219–248 (2008)
40. Carnaghan, C.: Business process modeling approaches in the context of process level audit risk assessment: An analysis and comparison. Int. J. Account. Inform. Syst. **7**, 170–240 (2006)
41. Lin, F.-R., Yang, M.-C., et al.: A generic structure for business process modeling. Bus. Process Manage. J. **8**(1), 19–41 (2002)

Integration of Risk Aspects into Business Process Modeling

Tobias Anton[✉], Richard Lackes, and Markus Siepermann

Faculty of Business, Economics and Social Sciences, Department of Business
Information Management, TU Dortmund University,
Otto-Hahn Str. 12, 44227 Dortmund, Germany
{Tobias.Anton, Richard.Lackes,
Markus.Siepermann}@tu-dortmund.de

Abstract. Regulatory rules force most enterprises to implement a risk management system with a detailed documentation of their risk situation. In parallel, business processes which can be source and target of risks are systematically documented. Hence, it seems obvious to combine both tasks. Despite research's long lasting focus on risk management and business process management, only few approaches exist that try to fully integrate risk aspects into business process models. Most methods consider risk management only partly. This paper therefore develops a comprehensive concept for the integration of risk aspects into business process modeling. It is based on the Business Process Model and Notation (BPMN) 2.0, that only needs to be extended carefully.

Keywords: BPMN · Business processes · Business process modeling · Risk management

1 Introduction

Business processes are the basis of any enterprise information system. Up to now, many enterprises invest in the documentation, analysis and enhancement of their processes following the mantra of ISO 9000 that only good processes can result in permanent good output. On the one hand, business processes define and generate the data to be managed and processed in enterprise information systems. On the other hand, business processes are a mapping of organizational structures and workflows. Apart from the process view, enterprise information systems have been extended by risk management applications reacting on legal requirements like the Sarbanes-Oxley Act in the US or the KonTraG in Germany, to name only a few. Business processes can provide valuable meta-information that can be used for risk management [7, 16]. An analysis of raw process data can already give hints on potential risks. In addition, business processes show relations and dependencies between different departments or partners that may lead to problems in case of a risk. Hence, it seems reasonable to connect business process management and risk management [7].

Therefore, during the past decade, many studies investigated in combining risk management and business process management [33]. Several authors proposed risk extensions to business process modeling notations that in general do not provide

© Springer International Publishing Switzerland 2016
M. Felderer et al. (Eds.): ERP Future 2015 - Research, LNBIP 245, pp. 46–61, 2016.
DOI: 10.1007/978-3-319-32799-0_4

elements to entirely integrate risk aspects into the models. However not one of the proposed extensions covers all relevant risk aspects and the extensions are not combinable. In this paper, we propose an extension to the Business Process Model and Notation (BPMN) 2.0 standard that overcomes the named problems. We have chosen this notation as it has a growing popularity in practice worldwide [27] and because it is an industry standard from the Object Management Group (OMG). BPMN does not only support process documentation, but also process automation. Among others, its advantage is the close relation to information technology which is also a critical success factor for risk management systems [17]. Extensions to the notation are carefully done by using existing elements whenever possible. In general, a company's business processes already exist as process models. Therefore, a fundamental change of a given notation is not useful. For this reason, we introduce an extension that enables practitioners to integrate risk aspects into existing process models without changing their structure. The integration can either be used to document and analyze risk-cause-and-effect chains or to unveil the relations between a process and its risks. With this approach existing modeling tools can be continued to be used and only need to be upgraded with a few visual elements and rule sets.

The remainder of this paper is organized as follows. Section 2 derives the requirements for risk-aware business process models from the risk-theoretic basics. In Sect. 3, a literature review checks these requirements against existing approaches. Section 4 introduces our new approach based on BPMN 2.0 that fully meets the requirements derived. The paper closes in Sect. 5 with a conclusion.

2 Requirements for Risk-Aware Business Process Modeling

2.1 Risks and Risk Events

In general, risk is the possibility that one or more events affect the achievement of firm objectives [8, 12]. Reasons for not achieving a planned outcome are the general uncertainty about states, future developments and the effect strength of factors influencing an enterprise's objectives. Commonly, uncertainty and incomplete information characterize the general situation of decision making [15]. Improving the information level can therefore be seen as a measure of risk reduction [31] which is important in the risk management stage of risk control. Beside uncertainty, a risk may result from the occurrence of negatively influencing events like natural hazards or fraud [6, 9]. Hence, we can differentiate between causes as a source for the emergence of risk and the effects in terms of not achieving objectives. In contrast to the level of information, which from a system-theoretic perspective describes a state, a risk event describes the change of a system state i.e. it is the trigger of a transformation process from an initial state into a resulting state [29].

Most common business process modeling notations offer to model activities, events and their relations. Because a risk itself has individual characteristics like impact and likelihood and as it is part of every business activity [4], a separate element to model risk seems reasonable for risk-aware business process modeling. In addition a separate risk symbol makes it easier to model interrelations between risks itself.

2.2   Impact and Likelihood

It is common to assess a risk by its impact and likelihood of occurrence [24]. If concrete values for impact and likelihood are missing, these might be simulated e.g. by Monte Carlo simulation. To fully cover a risk's relevance in a business process it therefore has to be possible to declare impact and likelihood of each modeled risk object in a risk-aware business process modeling notation.

2.3   Risk Ownership

It is a consensus in literature that in respect of a responsible and proper handling of risks it is necessary to assign a person in charge, the so called risk owner, for each risk [36]. If not, this may lead to a mistreatment or even a non-treatment of risk as nobody feels responsible. In general, two risk owners are conceivable. The person in charge of the unit where the risk arises or where it impacts. [29] We argue that the earlier a cause-and-effect chain between risks is influenced, the better and the easier a risk situation can be handled. Hence, the person in charge of that business unit where a risk arises should be the responsible risk owner [29]. An exception has to be made for risks that arise externally. The sources of these risks are outside the influence of the firm. As the firm has no control over the source, the risk owner should be the person in charge of that business unit of the firm where the risk effect impacts. Here, the risk owner has to take suitable measures to be prepared if the external risk occurs. Concluding, the possibility to define a risk owner for each risk is another requirement for risk-aware business process modeling.

2.4   Risk Cause-and-Effect Chains and Firm Environment

Risk events do not only influence system states but may also depend on, influence or trigger each other. Hence, static and dynamic relations between risk states, risks and risk events do exist. Furthermore, it requires a specific risk situation for a risk event to take effect. For example, if a firm is sourcing from international markets, it will be affected by a rising Dollar rate. But if it has long-term supplier contracts based on Euro, the risk of a rising Dollar rate does not affect the firm. The context and environmental factors are therefore of importance and should be considered when modeling risks in a process model.

Furthermore, risks can not only be a precondition for each other but can also increase or mitigate one another or influence each other's probability of occurrence. Between them, complex risk cause-and-effect chains (RCEC) exist [29]. Knowing these is key to a successful mitigation of risk [9]. The mitigation can be achieved either by reducing the risk's impact, its probability or by influencing its causal chain [26]. As every risk in a RCEC can be the cause for or the effect of other risks, a distinct classification of risks into causes and effects is not possible [19]. In addition RCEC may not only be sequential, as risks can be related to each other in different ways. For example different risks can lead to the same subsequent risk or two risks may be a precondition for another risk to occur. Furthermore risks can increase or decrease each other's impact and probability.

Because a risk's effect does not always follow immediately after its cause, time sequences are another important aspect of RCEC. Often a time lag between cause and effect exists. This time lag can be used to prepare for the effect during the risk control stage of the risk management process in order to decrease the risk impact.

As we can see, RCEC can be of high complexity. The knowledge of their various relations, logical connections and appearance in time is crucial for understanding impacts and therefore for developing mitigation strategies. Therefore a risk extension to business process modeling should be able to model these risk relations including their logical connections and influences.

2.5 Risk Measures and Control

Risk measures are business processes that are executed to mitigate or eliminate risks. They can address cause and effect of a risk by influencing their probability of occurrence or their impact. Or the functional relation is influenced by interrupting or manipulating the causal relation between cause and effect [29]. While a risk measure's objective is to influence risks positively, it is also possible that a measure triggers other risks, influences causal relations in a negative manner, or prevents activities from functioning in their normal state. Hence, a risk measure always has an effect on probability and impact of one or more risks. As risk measures interplay with risks and RCEC, they should be modeled too in order to get a holistic overview of the risk management activities in business process models and their interdependencies. Additionally, in order to measure when a risk occurs key figures have to be monitored. Hence, key figures and their thresholds in consideration of business goals need to be defined so that risks can be detected.

3 Literature Review

Suriadi et al. [33] give an extensive overview of the existing literature that aims for integrating risk management in business process management. In total, they identified 27 approaches until the year 2011 and classified seventeen approaches as supporting the design phase of risk-aware business process management with integrated risk constructs. We applied the same search method as of [33] and found two additional papers [18, 20]. In addition, we also analysed three non-english papers [5, 10, 25]. Table 1 summarizes all papers according to the requirements we derived in the previous section. For papers that do not base on a certain BPM language we use the term "generic". Because we do not aim for a comprehensive literature review, we mentioned only the first occurrence of a certain approach in this table. For following and extending papers we refer to Suriadi et al. [33].

The approaches of [1, 4, 34] do not extend business process modeling (BPM) by risks. Instead, they aim for simulating processes and analysing how processes are affected by uncertainties. In addition, they do not use common BPM languages.

Table 1. Related risk-aware business process modeling approaches

		Model	Risk/ Risk Event	Impact	Likelihood	Risk Owner	Risk Cause-and-Effect Chains	Risk maesures	Environmental Factors	Controls/ Goals
Asnar/Giogini	2008	Generic	x					x		
Bai et al.	2006	Generic	x		x					x
Betz et al.	2011	XML nets	x	x	x		(x)	x		
Brabänder/Ochs	2002	EPC	x	x	x	x		x		x
Cope et al.	2010	BPMN 1.1	x				x	x	x	x
Hengmith	2005	EPC	x		x					x
Herrmann/Herrmann	2006	UML	(x)	(x)	(x)	x		x		x
Jakoubi et al.	2007	Generic	x	x	x		(x)	x	x	x
Karagiannis et al.	2007	ADONIS	x	x	x	(x)				x
Lambert et al.	2006	IDEF	x							(x)
Marcinkowski/Kuciapski	2012	BPMN 2.0	x	x	x			x		
Meland and Gjære	2012	BPMN 2.0	(x)	(x)	(x)			(x)		
Mock and Corvo	2005	EPC	x	x	x	x	(x)			(x)
Neiger et al.	2006	VFPE/EPC	x						x	x
Panayiotou et al.	2010	PowerDesigner	(x)	x	x			(x)		x
Rieke/Winkelmann	2008	EPC	x					x		
Sienou et al.	2007	EPC	x	x	x		(x)	x	x	
Strecker et al.	2011	MEMO	x	x	x	x	x	x		x
Taylor et al.	2008	jBPM/JPDL	x	x	x					x
Weiß/Winkelmann	2011	SBPML	x	x	x	x	(x)	x		x
zur Muehlen/Rosemann	2005	EPC	x	x	x			x		x

The same holds for Bai et al. [2] who aim for optimally placing controls in business process models. The application of [14] is very specific (SOX and finance) and mainly uses annotations to specify risks in processes. [11] are focused on security in (ebusiness) processes. Therefore, they introduce the concept of security requirements that are checked during runtime so that risk mitigation actions can automatically be started to reduce the risk to an acceptable level.

The remaining approaches introduce a special object for risks, threats or risk events that is usually linked to the activities and attributed by the impact and likelihood of the risk. In addition to the risk object, [22] provide a new risk structure model that helps to define of what other risks a risk is composed of and how risks can be (sub-) categorized. [10] introduces two interesting advancements that influence the structure of a business model. He allows for modeling unwanted shortcuts in processes and the possibility of faultily branching after activities that may occur with certain likelihood. Interestingly, the responsibility for risks is seldom explicitly considered [5, 11, 14, 21, 30, 35] although the importance of defining responsibility is stated in the commonly used ERM frameworks. Even if risks are linked to activities that belong to a process owner, the process owner is not necessarily the owner of that risk. The connected risk may lie outside the process owner's sphere of influence but within another one's sphere who is therefore much more suitable to be the risk owner.

Cause-and-effect chains between risks can be modeled only in a few models with sometimes certain restrictions. In the approaches [13, 28] as well as [35], only sequential cause-and-effect chains can be modeled. In [22], those relations between risks are considered in the so-called risk state model and risk structure model but not in the business process model itself. In [7], the causal effects can be modeled directly in the business process model but they do not consider logical connections between risks. Instead, relations between risks and business elements are drawn in parallel. Also in [21], only sequential causal effects can be modeled. There, the risks are linked to functions. If a risk evokes another risk, the second risk is linked to the first risk and so on. If a risk affects two functions, the risk is colored and a copy of the risk is used and linked to the second function. Only the approach of [30] considers logical connections between risks. But there, business model elements (activities, resources) are always linked with risks by an unidirectional "contains"-relation from element to risk. This is an advantageous simplification for risk modeling, but does not cover the complex risk phenomenon in total.

Risk measures are considered by the majority of approaches. They are usually linked to the risk elements they are intended to mitigate. However, no approach takes into account, that risk measures do not only have an impact on risks but also on other parts of the business process. It is the environment of business processes and the situation when the process is executed that enables risks to take effect on process elements. This is explicitly taken into account by four approaches [7, 13, 23, 28]. However, if we understand risk situations or states of environmental factors as being some kind of risk, this can be modeled with the help of the introduced risk element without loss of information.

The control and monitoring phases are supported by the majority of approaches. They propagate to define key figures so that risks can be detected or monitored. In addition, some approaches allow for the explicit definition of business goals. [22] for example, provide the additional risk goal model that visualizes the impact of risks on business goals via a matrix.

All in all, there is no approach that completely covers all risk phenomena in total. The most mature approach so far is the one of [30] that uses only a few extensions to the basic modeling language. Unfortunately, beside the not completely convincing risk cause-and-effect chain modeling, they use the uncommon BPM language MEMO (Multi-perspective Enterprise Modeling). Also [35] cover many risk aspects. However, their extension is based on the little-known SBPML of [3] that bears many restrictions like only a few predefined activities, no logical connections, only sequential business processeses or variants of processes. Because of this, the potential to model complex risk cause-and-effect chains is low. The approaches of [13, 28] offer many opportunities for modeling risks in processes but lack from insufficient support of cause-and-effect chains and risk owners. Besides, as with [7], the approaches are not kept simple and use many new constructs. [21] only use a few additional constructs but because they double risks that affect different parts of the process the modeling RCEC becomes confusing. In addition, they mix causal effect chains and the controlling information of risk priority numbers. All relevant approaches can be divided into two groups: Either separate risk layers are used that have to be modeled with new constructs in addition to the standard process [7, 13, 22] or the risk part of the process cannot be separated properly from the standard process without diverging into pieces [7, 21, 28, 22]. Another issue of some approaches is that proprietary [24, 30, 35] or uncommon [4, 34] BPM languages are used that are not commonly accepted or unknown in practice. The work of [20] is adverse to all the other work mentioned before. They argue that it is not necessary to introduce new constructs to business process modeling languages because BPMN 2.0 brings sufficient constructs to handle the risk phenomenon in business process models. It is eminent to keep a modeling language simple and the number of constructs low [30]. But [20] mainly focus on modeling risks/threats in business processes and their mitigation activities. Other aspects of risk management like risk ownership, complex cause-and-effect chains and environmental factors are neglected. Therefore, we will show in the following how to model these risk phenomena with BPMN 2.0 and where the standard has to be carefully extended in order to cover all aspects.

4   Model Development

In this section, we introduce a comprehensive approach based on the widespread standard BPMN 2.0 that integrates the concept of risk into business process modeling. Instead of using different additional diagrams that capture the risk phenomena, we integrate risk phenomena directly into the existing diagrams. For this, we show how to reuse and extend existing BPMN elements for risk modeling and where and how it is necessary to introduce new elements. All risk related elements can be captured in a separate layer that can be switched on and off without affecting the structure of the process. The risk layer itself can also be read without the entire process. Only a few elements of the process layer (error events, resources related to risks) refer to both layers. Then, if the business process layer is switched off, the pure risk cause-and-effect chain becomes visible. Figure 1 shows the basic concepts for modeling risk in BPMN 2.0. We illustrate our approach with the goods receiving process that is expanded by new risk elements in Fig. 2.

4.1   Risks and Risk Cause-and-Effect Chains

The need for a risk element in business process modeling is a consensus in literature (see Table 1). [20] suggest to use error and escalation events to model risk events in BPMN. This bears several drawbacks. First of all, both elements are events but this is only one part of the risk phenomenon. Other important parts are the level of information and uncertainty (Sect. 2.1) as well as risk situations and environmental factors (Sect. 2.4). Secondly, risks may not only be errors in activities but may also originate from resources, external events etc. Thirdly, using existing elements hampers a clear distinction between the process model and the risk model. Therefore, we introduce an additional risk element depicted by an octagon (see Fig. 1) that for simplicity represents risks, risk events, risk situations or environmental factors. The distinction between these phenomena is realized by a property risk type. In addition, each risk is characterized by its impact and likelihood for a certain period of time.

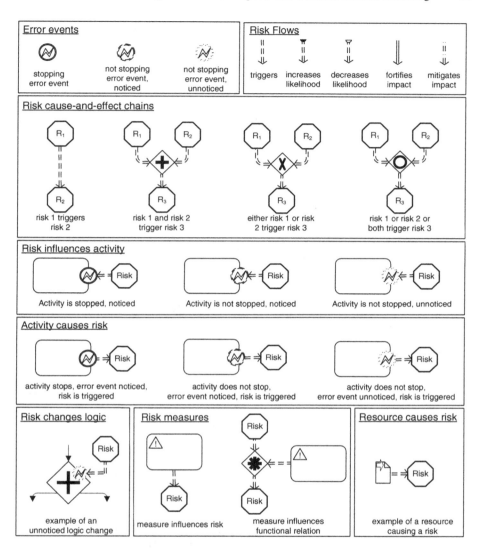

Fig. 1. Risk elements for the BPMN 2.0

Between risks (see Sect. 2), there are complex cause-and-effect chains. For example, the risk strike can cause labor shortage in the receiving department so that checks of delivered goods are omitted. To model the relations between risks in cause-and-effect chains, we recline to the concept of flows and introduce the concept of risk flows. A risk flow flowing from risk A to risk B means that A influences B or in other words increases or decreases B's impact and/or likelihood. To distinguish the different categories of influence, we use different attributes. If a risk A just triggers risk B, we use a dashed double line between A and B. If the likelihood of B is affected by A, we use a semicircle at the risk flow's source. For an increase of B's likelihood,

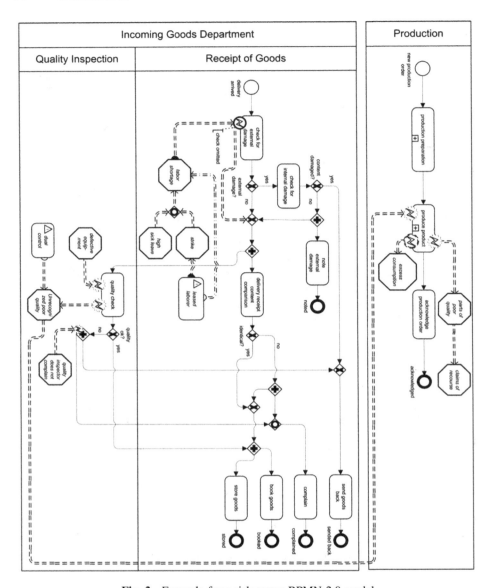

Fig. 2. Example for a risk-aware BPMN 2.0 model

the semicircle is filled. In Fig. 2 this can be seen between "labor shortage" and "check omitted". For a decrease, the semicircle is not filled. If B's impact is affected by A, we change the risk flow's style. If B's impact is fortified, we use a solid double line. If it is mitigated, we use a dashed and dotted double line. If risks are interrelated, the relations can also be recursive. The exact increase or decrease of impact or likelihood can be specified with the help of the risk flow's properties. Also a possible time delay between two risks can be documented via risk flow properties.

Within risk cause-and-effect chains, there are not only sequential but arbitrarily complex structures. That means one risk is not only caused by another. Instead, there may be logical relations between risks. For example, the labor shortage is not only caused by strike but also by high sick leave. In BPMN, such logical connections are modeled with the help of gateways (AND, OR, XOR) so that no new elements are needed. In our example, we place an OR-gateway between risks "strike" and "high sick leave" leading to risk "labor shortage".

We have to keep in mind that risk cause-and-effect chains just document the general relations between risks, i.e. how impact and likelihood are influenced. That means that if a preceding risk A occurs, the likelihood of a subsequent risk B may be positively influenced. It does not mean that if A occurs also B will certainly occur. If we explicitly want to model such a relation, we have to use the concept of properties for the risk flow that describe this certain cause-and-effect. Furthermore, risk B can also occur without risk A occurring before. For example, labor shortage influences the likelihood of the risk "check omitted" but the check of received goods can also be omitted apart from strike and labor shortage.

4.2 Risk and Business Process Activities

The risks and risk cause-and-effect chains described in the previous section may affect all parts of business processes, especially activities. Risks can stop or decelerate a process or even change the process structure and logic. For example, defective quality check equipment negatively influences the quality check activity (see swimlane quality inspection in Fig. 2). The process can be stopped if the equipment breaks down or can proceed if the defect keeps unrecognized and the equipment is just measuring faultily. If an activity is being stopped when a risk occurs, employees usually recognize the error. But if the activity does not stop, the risk occurrence may possibly keep unrecognized or will be recognized later. On the other hand, risks are caused when processing activities, e.g. the production of faulty parts. If an activity causes a risk, we are usually facing an unwanted error event of the activity that causes a risk. Error events are already part of BPMN 2.0. We use these error events for risks occurring within an activity that cause risks outside the activity. For this, an error event is attached to the activity and a risk flow between the error event and the caused risk is drawn (e.g. between error event of activity quality check and risk unrecognized poor quality). The concept of error events is also used for risks that affect activities. We attach an error event to the activity and draw a risk flow from risk to error event. This indicates that the risk affects the activity by causing an error (e.g. risk defective equipment affects activity quality check). The kind of error should be annotated to the error event directly.

4.3 Risk, Business Process Logic, and Other Process Elements

Error events in BPMN are always supposed to stop an activity. In contrast, this does not hold for risks as we discussed above. Therefore, we have to distinguish between interrupting and non-interrupting error events. For the latter case, [20] suggest to use escalation events that do not necessarily interrupt. The downside of escalation events is that they always demand for a report to the supervisor. In many cases, this might be intended but in many other cases employees are skilled enough to fight risks and do not need to report every single risk. Besides, risks may easily stay unrecognized if an activity is not interrupted. Thus, we have to distinguish between interruptive and non-interruptive error events, the latter of which can be recognized or unrecognized. For non-interruptive events, BPMN uses dashed circles that we reuse for error events. To distinguish between noticed and unnoticed events, we use the dashed circle for noticed and a dotted circle for unnoticed risks. For example, the defect of the quality check equipment is unnoticed and does not stop the quality check activity while labor shortage obviously affects the check of delivered goods. The way how an activity is affected by risks can be defined via properties (impact, likelihood) of the incoming flow.

We suggest distinguishing between incoming and outgoing error events of an activity because an incoming risk first affects the activity and causes changes in the activity's procedure. Not till then, these changes cause other risks. That means that there is a relation between incoming and outgoing risks that can be described in more detail in sub-processes. But to clarify that incoming and outgoing risks do not have a direct connection, different error events should be used. If we switch off the business process layer, then the internal relation between the two error events is realized by risk flows from incoming to outgoing error events. In our example, the defective quality check equipment affects the quality check. Therefore, goods cannot be tested correctly so that the poor quality of goods keeps unnoticed. This is an internal relation of the quality check. But the risk that the poor quality is unnoticed can also occur independently of the quality check equipment. For this, we separate the incoming from the outgoing error event. If risks cause different errors in an activity, we suggest to model different error events so that it is possible to distinguish them.

Only if a risk that affects an activity directly causes another risk, the error event should have incoming and outgoing risk flows. Let us again have a look at the example in Fig. 2. The labor shortage provokes that the goods are not checked concerning damage. Because of this, all goods are directly classified as undamaged. Therefore, the error event of the activity "check for external damage" has an incoming as well as an outgoing flow that skips the activity and directly leads to the "no"-branch.

As we can see, risks do not only affect activities but may also result in structural changes. It is conceivable that additional flows accrue, that flows are omitted or skipped or that risks change the logic of a gateway e.g. from "AND" to "OR". Skipping of flows can easily be realised by using a risk flow that starts from an error event and points to that position in the process flow where the disrupted process continues. In our example, this case accrues when the activity "check for external damage" is affected by the risk "labor shortage" so that the check is skipped to the "no"-branch. Concerning the change in process logic, this risk phenomenon cannot be captured without changing the original business process. Because we aim for keeping the original process untouched and modeling just an additional risk layer, we have to extend the syntax of BPMN. Usually, error events can only be attached to activities. We suggest attaching error events to any business process element that can be affected by risks. Then, according to our considerations above, a risk flow from a risk to the attached error event shows that the element is affected by risk. A flow from the attached error event indicates that the induced error causes risks or changes somewhere else. Concerning resources, attaching an error event for example may indicate that the quality or quantity of that resource is influenced. The exact influence is again documented via properties of risk flow and error event. Now, if a risk changes the logic or structure of a gateway, we attach an error event to the gateway. Then, the changed logic can either be described by properties of the error event or in more detail via sub-processes. In our example, we can find the risk that an inspector does not complain about the poor quality of goods. This risk affects the logic of the AND-gateway. Usually, activities "complain about quality" and "send back goods" should both be processed. But because of the risk, the flow from gateway to activity "complain about quality" is omitted so that there will be no complaint.

4.4   Risk Measures

Risk measures aim for fighting risks and mitigating their impact on the business. They are not part of the normal business process but of processes executed by risk management. As such, they can be modeled as normal activities but within the risk layer of business processes. We therefore explicitly mark an activity as being a risk measure by adding an exclamation mark surrounded by a triangle to the BPMN task element. However, a risk measure should be categorized concerning its general strategy (avoidance, mitigation, transfer) via property. If a measure should fight a risk concerning its impact or likelihood, the risk flow runs from measure to risk. The same categories for risk flows are applied as between risks. In our example, a risk measure against the labor shortage in the receiving department is to hire leased laborer. This reduces impact as well as likelihood of labor shortage in the department. However, responses may not only fight risks but also promote other risks at the same time. The employment of leased laborer for example bears the downside that the likelihood of the risk strike increases.

A measure does not only have an impact on likelihood and impact but also on the functional relations between risk causes and effects. That means the measure changes the risk flow of the cause-and-effect chain between risks. We handle this phenomenon as follows: We insert a complex gateway into the risk flow between two risks and also a risk flow from risk measure to the complex gateway. Then, properties of the complex gateways can describe how the measure influences the risk flow and therefore the relation between the risks.

4.5   Risk Owner and Risk Handler

We have to distinguish two different roles concerning risks: Risk owner and risk handler. The risk owner is responsible for a risk because it originates in the risk owner's sphere of influence. The risk handler is fighting the risk or has to deal with the risk. We suggest to use BPMN's concept of swimlanes for risk ownership in the same way that it is used for process ownership. Risks should be documented in the swimlane of that process owner who is responsible for the sphere where the risk originates. But risks are not limited to sectors or divisions. A risk emerging in one department like the not sufficiently checked shipment in the department quality check can cause other risks in other departments like excess consumption in production. Or because of the poor quality, a machine does not work properly and produces parts of poor quality that break down at the customer. This again may induce claims of recourse. While the risk of not detecting poor quality of goods originates in the quality check department, the other risks emerge in production but are caused by the first risk. Risk owner of the risk of not detecting poor quality is the quality check department but risk handler is the production department. Thus, recording and documenting risk cause-and-effect chains helps to fairly assign risks and their consequences to those who are really responsible. For a further and more detailed description of the responsibility, we can use the properties of the risk element. Elsewise, we have to introduce new business process elements for departments or persons in charge where risks are assigned to.

5   Conclusion

The documentation of a firm's risks is as crucial for risk management as the documentation of business processes so that it seems beneficial to combine both tasks. In this paper, we therefore presented a comprehensive approach that integrates risk concepts into business process modeling with BPMN 2.0. The main objective was that firms can model risks using their already existing business process models without any change in the business process structure. This was achieved by introducing a separate risk layer that can be switched on and off. Extensions of BPMN are introduced such that risks can easily be identified when viewing the process and risk model together. But the number of extensions is kept low so that the reader as well as the modeler is not confused by too many new symbols.

The advantages of such an approach are obvious. If business process model and risk model are viewed together, the interrelations between business processes and risks become apparent. If the risk layer is viewed isolatedly, the complex nature of a firm's risk cause-effect chains can be seen and analyzed. With the help of the risk layer, the risk situation of a firm becomes clearly visible. It is not only possible to document the logic between risks themselves, between risks and the process structure, impact, and likelihood, it is also possible to document risks that change the logic or the structure of a process. Thus, risk managers get a complete risk map of the entire process landscape. This enables them to analyze which areas or units of their firm are jeopardized by risks to what extent so that they get a decision support where to install counter measures. Such risk measures can be taken once to mitigate certain risks, or they can be installed permanently. This leads to a standardized risk monitoring and improves the maturity of the firm's risk management system.

Based on the business processes and the quantitative documentation of risks and their interrelations, simulation studies can be implemented to get a deeper insight into the risk behavior of a firm's processes. With the help of simulation studies, also prognoses about future risk developments are conceivable. However, the step to automatize risk simulations on the basis of process and risk models is not well defined yet. Before, some work has to be done in the future. First of all, the approach has to be described formally to alter the BPMN meta-model as it is proposed by [33]. Then, connections between properties of the risk model and a suitable simulation model have to be defined as well as suitable key figures.

Some other limitations also remain. Our approach is not generic and extends only BPMN 2.0. A next step will be to generalize the approach, splitting it into a presentation model and a formal logical model so that it can be used with other business process modeling notations like e.g. EPC. In addition, the approach is not empirically tested yet. For the future, we plan to evaluate the approach with partnering firms to test its applicability, its benefit, and its acceptance in firms.

References

1. Asnar, Y., Giorgini, P.: Analyzing business continuity through a multi-layers model. In: Dumas, M., Reichert, M., Shan, M.-C. (eds.) BPM 2008. LNCS, vol. 5240, pp. 212–227. Springer, Heidelberg (2008)
2. Bai, X., Padman, R., Krishnan, R.: On Risk management in business process design. Technical report, The H. John Heinz III School of Public Policy and Management, Carnegie Mellon University (2006). http://heinz.cmu.edu/research/296full.pdf
3. Becker, J., Weiß, B., Winkelmann, A.: Developing a business process modeling language for the banking sector – a design science approach. In: Proceedings of the 15th Americas Conference on Information Systems, San Francisco, pp. 1–12 (2009)
4. Betz, S., Hickl, S., Oberweis, A.: Risk-aware business process modeling and simulation using XML nets. In: Proceedings of the 2011 IEEE Conference on Commerce and Enterprise Computing, pp. 349–356 (2011)
5. Brabänder, E., Ochs, H.: Analyse und Gestaltung prozessorientierter Risikomanagement systeme mit Ereignisgesteuerten Prozessketten. In: Nüttgens, M., Rump, F. (eds.) Geschäftsprozessmanagement mit Ereignisgesteuerten Prozessketten – EPK 2002. Proceedings des GI Workshops und Arbeitskreistreffens, pp. 17–35 (2002)
6. Carter, R.L., Crockford, G. N.: The development and scope of risk management. In: Pountney, B. (eds.) Handbook of Risk Management, Kingston upon Thames, pp. 1.1–01–1.1–21 (1999)
7. Cope, E.W., Kuster, J., Etzweiler, D., Deleris, L., Ray, B.: Incorporating risk into business process models. IBM J. Res. Develop. 54, 4:1–4:13 (2010)
8. COSO: Enterprise Risk Management - Integrated Framework. Executive Summary (2004). http://coso.org/documents/COSO_ERM_ExecutiveSummary.pdf
9. Gleißner, W.: Identifikation, Messung und Aggregation von Risiken. In: Gleißner, W., Meier, G. (eds.) Wertorientiertes Risiko-Management für Industrie und Handel, pp. 111–137. Gabler, Wiesbaden (2001)
10. Hengmith, L.: Geschäftsprozessmodellierung und -simulation als Hilfsmittel zum Management operationaler Risiken. Bank. Inf. Technol. 2, 17–29 (2005)
11. Herrmann, P., Herrmann, G.P.: Security requirement analysis of business processes. Electron. Commer. Res. 6(3–4), 305–335 (2006)
12. International Standards Organization: ISO 31000:2009 Risk Management-Principles and Guidelines (2009)
13. Jakoubi, S., Tjoa, S., Quirchmayr, G.: ROPE: a methodology for enabling the risk-aware modelling and simulation of business processes. In: Österle, H., Schelp, J., Winter, R. (eds.) Proceedings of the Fifteenth European Conference on Information Systems (ECIS 2007), pp. 1596–1607. University of St. Gallen, St. Gallen (2007)

14. Karagiannis, D., Mylopoulos, J., Schwab, M.: Business process-based regulation compliance: the case of the Sarbanes-Oxley act. In: Sutcliffe, A., Jalote, P. (eds.) Proceedings of the Fifteenth IEEE International Conference on Requirements Engineering (RE 2007), pp. 315–321. IEEE Computer Society, Los Alamitos (2007)
15. Knight, F.H.: Risk, Uncertainty and Profit. University of Chicago Press, Chicago and London (1971)
16. Lambert, J., Jennings, R., Joshi, N.: Integration of risk identification with business process models. Syst. Eng. 9(3), 187–198 (2006)
17. Li, L.: Study on the application of information technology in enterprise risk management. In: Proceedings of the 2013 International Conference on Quality, Reliability, Risk, Maintenance, and Safety Engineering (QR2MSE), pp. 2146–2150 (2013)
18. Marcinkowski, B., Kuciapski, M.: A business process modeling notation extension for risk handling. In: Cortesi, A., Chaki, N., Saeed, K., Wierzchoń, S. (eds.) CISIM 2012. LNCS, vol. 7564, pp. 374–381. Springer, Heidelberg (2012)
19. März, O.: Die Kalkulierbarkeit des Risikos. Frankfurt am Main (1948)
20. Meland, P., Gjære, A.: Representing threats in BPMN 2.0. In: Proceedings of the 2012 Seventh International Conference on Availability, Reliability and Security (ARES), Prague, pp. 542–550 (2012)
21. Mock, R., Corvo, M.: Risk analysis of information systems by event process chains. Int. J. Crit. Infrastruct. IJCIS 1, 247–257 (2005)
22. zur Muehlen, M., Rosemann, M.: Integrating risks in business process models. In: ACIS 2005 Proceedings, Paper 50, Sydney (2005)
23. Neiger, D., Churliov, L., zur Muehlen, M., Rosemann, M.: Integrating risks in business process models with value focused process engineering. In: Proceedings of the Fourteenth European Conference on Information Systems (ECIS 2006), Association for Information Systems (2006). http://aisel.aisnet.org/ecis2006/122/
24. Panayiotou, N., Oikonomitsios, S., Athanasiadou, C., Gayialis, S.: Risk assessment in virtual enterprise networks: a process-driven internal audit approach. In: Ponis, S. (ed.) Managing Risk in Virtual Enterprise Networks: Implementing Supply Chain Principles, pp. 290–312. IGI Global, Hershey (2010)
25. Rieke, T., Winkelmann, A.: Modellierung und Management von Risiken. Ein prozessorientierter Risikomanagement-Ansatz zur Identifikation und Behandlung von Risiken in Geschäftsprozessen. Wirtschaftsinformatik 5, 346–356 (2008)
26. Romeike, F.: Der Prozess der Risikosteuerung und –kontrolle. In: Romeike, F., Finke, R.B. (eds.) Erfolgsfaktor Risikomanagement 3.0, 3rd edn, pp. 235–243. Gabler, Wiesbaden (2003)
27. Schultz, M., Radloff, M.: Modeling concepts for internal controls in business processes – an empirically grounded extension of BPMN. In: Sadiq, S., Soffer, P., Völzer, H. (eds.) BPM 2014. LNCS, vol. 8659, pp. 184–199. Springer, Heidelberg (2014)
28. Sienou, A., Lamine, E., Karduck, A., Pingaud, H.: Conceptual model of risk: towards a risk modelling language. In: Weske, M., Hacid, M.-S., Godart, C. (eds.) WISE 2007. LNCS, vol. 4832, pp. 118–129. Springer, Heidelberg (2014)
29. Siepermann, M.: Risikokostenrechnung. E. Schmidt, Berlin (2008)
30. Strecker, S., Heise, D., Frank, U.: RiskM: a multi-perspective modeling method for IT risk assessment. Inf. Syst. Front. 13(4), 595–611 (2011)
31. Streitfeld, L.: Grundlagen und Probleme der betriebswirtschaftlichen Risikotheorie. Gabler, Wiesbaden (1973)
32. Stroppi, L.J.R., Chiotti, O., Villarreal, P.D.: Extending BPMN 2.0: method and tool support. In: Dijkman, R., Hofstetter, J., Koehler, J. (eds.) BPMN 2011. LNBIP, vol. 95, pp. 59–73. Springer, Heidelberg (2011)

33. Suriadi, S., Weiß, B., Winkelmann, A., ter Hofstede, A., Adams, M.: Current research in risk-aware business process management – overview, comparison and gap analysis. Commun. Assoc. Inf. Syst. CAIS **34**, 933–984 (2014)
34. Taylor, P., Godino, J., Majeed, B.: Use of fuzzy reasoning in the simulation of risk events in business processes. In: Proceedings of the Twenty Second European Conference on Modelling and Simulation (ECMS 2008), pp. 25–30 (2008). http://www.scs-europe.net/conf/ecms2008/ecms2008%20CD/ecms2008%20pdf/ECMS2008.pdf
35. Weiß, B., Winkelmann, A.: Developing a process-oriented notation for modeling operational risks — a conceptual metamodel approach to operational risk management in knowledge intensive business processes within the financial industry. In: Proceedings of the Forty-Fourth Hawaii International Conference on Systems Science (HICSS 2011), pp. 1–10. IEEE Computer Society, Los Alamitos (2011)
36. Whylie, K., Gaedicke, C., Shahbodaghlou, F., Ganjeizadeh, F.: A risk analysis and mitigation methodology for infrastructure projects. J. Supply Chain Oper. Manag. **12**(2), 50–67 (2014)

Towards Rigid Actor Assignment in Dynamic Workflows

Christa Illibauer[(✉)], Thomas Ziebermayr, and Verena Geist

Software Competence Center Hagenberg GmbH, Hagenberg, Austria
{christa.illibauer,thomas.ziebermayr,verena.geist}@scch.at
http://www.scch.at

Abstract. Compared to business processes in other business domains, dynamic workflows in disaster management need a rather rigid allocation of work to actors. The work schedule must conform to available resources and their skills. Moreover, to ensure that each actor is able to quickly start working and to complete pieces of work rapidly, work must be distributed evenly. This also reduces the overall waiting time, which is an important issue in disaster management. Additionally, each actor should only have few tasks assigned at any point in time in order to be able to reliably perform critical tasks, without being overburdened. As conventional Business Process Management (BPM) tools do not fully meet these requirements, we provide an additional layer to BPM tools, the so-called Dynamic Resource Allocation (DRA) component.

Keywords: Dynamic resource allocation · Business process modelling · Dynamic workflows · Disaster management

1 Introduction

Dynamic workflows that are typically applied in disaster management require a rather rigid allocation of work to actors compared to business processes in other business domains. The work schedule must comply with the available resources, skills of each individual actor (or emergency team member), and the number of existing team members. Furthermore, it is especially important that work is distributed evenly so that each team member can quickly start working and is able to rapidly complete pieces of work. Thereby, the overall waiting time is automatically reduced, which is the key element in disaster management. In addition, at any time each team member has only assigned few tasks, which the member is able to perform without being overstrained in order to ensure that each task will be performed reliably.

The research reported in this paper has been partly supported by the Austrian Ministry for Transport, Innovation and Technology, the Federal Ministry of Science, Research and Economy, and the Province of Upper Austria in the frame of the COMET center SCCH.

© Springer International Publishing Switzerland 2016
M. Felderer et al. (Eds.): ERP Future 2015 - Research, LNBIP 245, pp. 62–69, 2016.
DOI: 10.1007/978-3-319-32799-0_5

However, existing Business Process Management (BPM) tools do not realize precisely these requirements. Most BPM tools offer static assignment of a task to a user group at design time and at runtime the task is automatically instantiated and assigned to each member of that group. Just one member of the group can pick that task for processing, which means that the task is no longer visible to the other group members. Only the member who has picked the task is allowed to start, perform, and complete it.

In this paper, we address the special resource allocation requirements of dynamic workflows in disaster management within our project called INDYCO (*Integrated Dynamic Decision Support System Component for Disaster Management Systems*). Different aspects of the INDYCO project have already been described in [1–3]. Now we propose a rigid actor assignment concept for dynamic workflows by adapting an existing BPM tool.

The paper is organised as follows. In Sect. 2, we briefly describe the general procedure of disaster management and discuss the current problem of resource allocation in business process modelling languages in a general way. After presenting some related work in Sect. 3, we elaborate on the requirements for dynamic resource allocation in disaster management and provide our approach for dynamically assigning actors to user tasks in Sect. 4. Section 5 evaluates the suggested solution using a real scenario of a flood forecasting system. Finally, we conclude the paper and show an outlook to future work in Sect. 6.

2 Preliminaries and Problem

2.1 General Procedure of Disaster Management

A Continuous Situation Awareness (CSA) component permanently analyses actual sensor data and, if necessary, provides warnings to the corresponding decision makers (see [2]). The decision makers can approve these warnings under inclusion of weather prediction or geographical data. Thereupon, a dynamic workflow system is triggered with the following demands: In the graphical user interface (GUI) of the related operation controllers all team members are displayed and when a process is executed, additionally, all tasks of this process are illustrated in the GUI. The operation controllers can then assign the related team member to each task by drag and drop. As a consequence, the assigned member can see the task instance on their mobile device when the task is instantiated, i.e. when process control reaches that task.

2.2 Common Approach to Actor Assignment

We discuss the ineligibility of the common approach for assigning actors to user tasks in dynamic workflows by using the widespread modelling language Business Process Model and Notation (BPMN) [4] as an example.

A BPMN process model basically consists of different flow elements, such as start and end event nodes, diverging and converging gateways, and activity (task or sub-process) nodes. Task nodes (or tasks) are nodes where an indivisible piece of work has to be performed by a single process participant. BPMN distinguishes between different task types (i.e. manual task, service task, user task, script task, send task, receive task, and business rule task), but for the assignment of actors in this work only user tasks are relevant. BPMN provides a further concept of swimlanes, including the elements *Pool* and *Lane*, which could be relevant for actor assignment. A pool is not intended for the assignment of an actor or a group of actors to a user task. However, the lane concept can be used for group assignment ("**Lanes** are often used for such things as internal roles (e.g., Manager, Associate)" [4, p. 305]).

We forgo a deeper introduction to BPMN as mainly user tasks and lanes are relevant for our purpose and refer to [4] for further details.

The assignment of actors to user tasks in BPMN is done statically at design time by (i) either setting the property *resources* of a user task (inherited from the base class *Activity*), which provides the possibility to define particular actors or groups of actors that are allowed to perform an instance of this task node or by (ii) modelling a pool that contains one or more lanes representing the groups/roles that are allowed to process the included user tasks. Furthermore, BPMN defines the instance attribute *actualOwner* for user tasks, which represents the actor that picked the task instance for execution at runtime.

In many cases, the possibilities of BPMN for actor assignment may be sufficient but not for special domains such as disaster management, where we need to *dynamically* assign a task to one particular actor. Thus, using the static assignment possibilities is ineligible or can be even dangerous when handling safety-critical situations, because in an organisation a lot of business process models exist and over time the roles as well as the employees change. For each modification of the roles, all business processes must be reviewed and adapted to the new roles. The static assignment of a task to only a certain actor is anyway dangerous because the process would wait infinitely in case of unavailability of this actor, e.g. when the actor is on vacation or has changed their job.

3   Related Work

Several theoretical approaches discuss the problem of dynamic resource allocation, however, most of them address this issue with the goal of *optimizing* resource allocations in different domains, e.g. [5,6]. Further approaches in the domain of business process and workflow management suggest, for example, a general approach for actor modelling in business processes [7] that supports different layers of abstraction to increase expressiveness or propose the addition of a team concept to today's workflow management systems [8]. However, they do not meet the requirements for reliable execution of safety-critical tasks in disaster management and are not integrated in existing BPM software as well.

Although there are some concrete approaches towards dynamic assignment of actors in business processes, these approaches are also not sufficient for our purpose. For example, some BPM tools [9,10] provide the opportunity to dynamically assign actors to task instances by using process variables, which are defined at design time and set at runtime. However, since process variables belong to the entire process instance and an activity (task) does not have own variables, this does not meet our requirements for a reliable resource allocation approach suitable for disaster management. A similar concept is used in [11] but provides a special performer data field/parameter.

In [12] input and output data associations are used instead of process variables, which are also defined at design time.

A further BPM tool [13] provides so-called actor filters, which have to be implemented and deployed with the process. At runtime an assigned task can be released and later be assigned to another actor by using the actor filter. However, after having been released, the task is handled as a pending task that is seen by all group members, which does not comply with our requirements.

Another possibility is presented in [10] by defining two properties *activiti:assignee* and *activiti:candidateUsers*, which are also set at design time. However, this only provides an opportunity to limit the members for whom a task is visible but does not offer a particular dynamic assignment as we need it.

In [14] a group/role is not statically assigned to a task in a process model but a mapping of roles to business activities is defined and applied at runtime. Nevertheless, this mapping is also static and refers to defined groups of users, thus providing no support for assigning a particular actor to a task.

4   Dynamic Actor-to-User Task Assignment Approach

One of the responsibilities in the INDYCO project to realize a dynamic decision support component for disaster management systems was to develop a rigid actor assignment method for demonstrating dynamic workflows. Our envisioned dynamic workflow system allows to dynamically adapt workflows by using the so-called *mini story* concept. A mini story is a semantically logical unit for complex workflow construction, modelled in BPMN (see [15]).

As we can see from the problem description and related work, a more flexible assignment approach for actors to user tasks is necessary for dynamic workflows, preferably one that can be done at runtime, referring to the instance of a certain task and not to the static task node in the business process model. Furthermore, the process engine, which is responsible for executing business processes with all their tasks, has to be designed for this requirement. Normally, the process engine offers an enabled user task instance to all actors belonging to the group that was statically assigned to that user task node in the process model. One of these actors can pick the task instance for execution, whereby this task instance is no longer visible to the other actors of the group. When the executing actor completes work on the task instance, the process engine changes its state to completed and in turn provides instance(s) of the subsequent task(s) of the process model to appropriate actors.

Based on our requirements, the question rose whether we should implement our own process engine, which is naturally able to handle dynamic actor assignment to user tasks, or if we should adapt an existing one. Apart from insufficient resources and lack of time for an own implementation, we decided to select one of a variety of existing process engines, offering the advantage that an existing process engine is already tested and widely used, and thus less error-prone than a new implementation would be. Another persuasive criterion was that dynamic actor assignment to user tasks is our only missing requirement of existing process engines, and this feature can be added with acceptable effort.

For our solution, we use the JBoss application server (version 7.1.1 final) (jBPM) for demonstrating dynamic workflows. However, the following discussion can also be applied to other BPM software, especially process engines which mainly provide static actor assignment to user tasks.

In disaster management, a task should be assigned to a particular actor that is actually available, because the actor has to start working immediately. Furthermore, the operation controllers will only allocate one or few tasks at a certain time to an emergency team member, which the member can perform promptly to not hinder the process flow. Otherwise, when each task is sent to all persons in a certain group, the team members would be confused about the plenty of tasks on their mobile devices and might hesitate to pick one of them. Furthermore, user task assignments in the area of disaster management are in principle rather fixed (to individual and available resources).

The opportunity to dynamically assign an actor to a task provided by JBoss and other BPM software [9,10] is to define a process variable for each process model at design time and to get or set this variable at runtime. For example, we can set this variable for each process instance to a certain actor (performer) of one task, but whenever we reset the process variable to another actor, who is intended to perform another task, the previous value is lost.

To our application logic, which uses the jBPM process engine, we now add an additional layer, the so-called *Dynamic Resource Allocation* (DRA) component (see Fig. 1), which is responsible for the (i) starting of mini stories, selected by decision makers, (ii) dynamic actor assignment, and (iii) completion of finished task instances. Whenever a decision maker approves a received warning, he/she can start several predefined mini stories to react to this warning, whereupon our DRA component instructs the process engine to start those mini stories. As a result, new process instances are created and executed. Each mini story is assigned to a particular emergency team, whose team leader can now dynamically assign a task of this process instance to a specific emergency team member, who has to perform this very task (see also Sect. 5). This assignment of an actor to a task is stored in a database. As at this point in time the tasks of the process are not yet instantiated, the assignment is to a certain extent static but dynamic to the running process instance. For this reason, we need to know, which tasks belong to which mini story and, therefore, have to also store this information.

During process execution, the task service, a part of the process engine, always delivers new instances of those tasks which are reached by the process control. The DRA component checks whether an actor is already assigned to those tasks and, if so, delivers the tasks to the Middleware, which in turn delivers them to the assigned emergency team member's mobile device. To guarantee correct process execution, we also force the process engine to start each task.

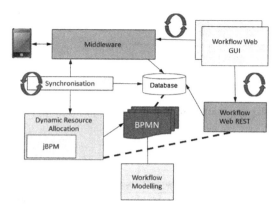

Fig. 1. Architecture overview

Finally, an emergency team member can complete an assigned task when all required work is done, which leads to setting the corresponding state of the task in the database. Thereupon, the DRA component forces the process engine to complete this task and the process execution provides the next task(s) of the mini story to be performed. Again, the DRA component delivers the task instance(s) until the process instance reaches its end.

5   Evaluation

In this section, we evaluate our solution for dynamic actor assignment to tasks. For that purpose we use the prototypical flood forecasting system for small catchment areas, which is able to dynamically and rapidly react to changing situations (with regard to the general procedure of disaster management). This prototype, which involves a real scenario, has successfully been evaluated at the Upper Austrian firefighters association within a demonstration.

As an example we provide the mini story *Dam Protection/Recovery*, which is illustrated in Fig. 2. The example depicts that a mini story is an own business process model (comprising only few activities, gateways, and events), which is a semantically logical unit, intended to define one specific measure that can be considered under certain circumstances, in our case in disaster management. The mini story describes the actions, which must be performed for protection and recovery of dams. Whenever the decision makers decide to take the measure, an instance of that mini story will be created and started.

The GUI presents all measures (the started mini stories), which were taken by the decision makers (see left side of Fig. 3). Each mini story can either be collapsed or expanded; in the expanded view, all tasks of that mini story are shown. Furthermore, in the GUI of the related operation controllers, all members of the assigned emergency team are displayed (see right side of Fig. 3). The operation controllers can assign a related team member to a task by drag and drop, whereby the colour of the actor icon next to the task changes (cf. Fig. 3).

Fig. 2. Example of a mini story (Dam protection/Recovery)

Fig. 3. Dynamic Actor Assignment

All in all, the demonstration at the Upper Austrian firefighters association showed that yet sensitive domains like disaster management can be supported by software systems and that the graphical presentation is able to support decision makers and give significant information to emergency team leaders (see [2]).

6   Conclusion

In this paper, we discussed the problem concerning dynamic resource allocation in general and in particular in existing BPM tools, whereby our attention focused on dynamic workflows in disaster management. We pointed out that existing BPM tools do not meet the requirements of rigid actor assignment in this domain.

By proposing an additional layer to existing BPM tools we enabled dynamic actor-to-user task assignment and showed how this extension can be implemented. Our solution suggests to include additional database tables, configure the BPM tool with available actors, use general role names (which are not likely to change over years), and implement the logic that a task instance may only be propagated when an available and authorized actor has been assigned.

The entire prototype was successfully evaluated within a demonstration at the Upper Austrian firefighters association. The proposed solution now enables fire brigade related information being built from data and supports decision makers and emergency team leaders in dynamically allocating significant tasks. In particular, the demonstration pointed out that even such sensitive areas as disaster management can be supported by software systems using the proposed rigid actor assignment in dynamic workflows.

Acknowledgements. The research leading to these results has received funding from the ERA-NET EraSME program under the Austrian grant agreement No. 836684, project INDYCO. This publication has been written within the project *AdaBPM* (No. 842437), which is funded by FFG.

References

1. Thalheim, B., Tropmann-Frick, M., Ziebermayr, T.: Application of generic workflows for disaster management. In: Information Modelling and Knowledge Bases XXV (EJC 2013), pp. 64–81 (2013)
2. Freudenthaler, B., Stumptner, R.: Adaptive flood forecasting for small catchment areas. In: Moreno-Díaz, R., Pichler, F., Quesada-Arencibia, A. (eds.) EUROCAST 2015. LNCS, vol. 9520, pp. 211–218. Springer, Heidelberg (2015). doi:10.1007/978-3-319-27340-2_27
3. Pichler, M., Leber, D.: On the formalization of expert knowledge: a disaster management case study. In: DEXA 2014, pp. 149–153 (2014)
4. BPMN: Business Process Model and Notation (BPMN) version 2.0.2 (2013). http://www.omg.org/spec/BPMN/2.0.2/. Accessed on 26 August 2015
5. Bertsimas, D., Gupta, S., Lulli, G.: Dynamic resource allocation: a flexible and tractable modeling framework. Eur. J. Oper. Res. **236**(1), 14–26 (2014)
6. Krakow, L.W., Rabiet, L., Zou, Y., Iooss, G., Chong, E.K., Rajopadhye, S.: Optimizing dynamic resource allocation. Procedia Comput. Sci. **29**, 1277–1288 (2014)
7. Natschläger, C., Geist, V.: A layered approach for actor modelling in business processes. Bus. Process Manag. J. **19**, 917–932 (2013)
8. van der Aalst, W.M., Kumar, A.: A reference model for team-enabled workflow management systems. Data Knowl. Eng. **38**(3), 335–363 (2001)
9. jBPM: Assign user or group dynamically to workflow (2014). https://groups.google.com/forum/#!topic/jbpm-development/upLMAt9zsB4. Accessed on 20 May 2015
10. Activiti: Dynamic assignment (2011). http://forums.activiti.org/content/dynamic-assignment. Accessed on 20 May 2015
11. TIBCO:Using a performer data field or parameter to dynamically define a participant (2015). https://docs.tibco.com/pub/activematrix_bpm/3.0.0/doc/html/GUID-225A26E2-75F9-4228-A7D4-05E13F3FBFC4.html. Accessed on 20 May 2015
12. ORACLE: BPM 11g - dynamic task assignment with multi-level organization units (2012). http://www.ateam-oracle.com/bpm-11g-dynamic-task-assignment-with-multi-level-organization-units/. Accessed on 20 May 2015
13. BonitaSoft: Dynamic human task group or user assigment (2015). http://community.bonitasoft.com/groups/usage-operation-6x/dynamic-human-task-group-or-user-assigment. Accessed on 20 May 2015
14. IBM:Dynamically retrieve and map human task information with WebSphere BPM v6.2 (2011). http://www.ibm.com/developerworks/websphere/library/techarticles/1106_gu/1106_gu.html. Accessed on 20 May 2015
15. Tropmann-Frick, M., Thalheim, B., Leber, D., Liehr, C., Czech, G.: Generic workflows - A utility to govern disastrous situations. In: Information Modelling and Knowledge Bases XXVI (EJC 2014), pp. 417–428 (2014)

Enterprise Systems and Solution Providers

Towards a Generic Resource Booking Management System

Michael Owonibi[✉], Eleonora Petzold, and Birgitta Koenig-Ries

Institute of Computer Science, Friedrich Schiller University, Jena, Germany
{michael.owonibi,eleonora.petzold,
birgitta.koenig-ries}@uni-jena.de

Abstract. Resource booking (the act of reserving of resources in advance) is an important component of planning-related activities. Typically, this is managed by a Booking Management System (BMS) which aims at controlling the access of people to resources at a specified future time. However, an issue common to BMSs is that they are typically modelled and developed to tightly fit the requirements of some specific contexts (use cases). This can lead to lack of reusability of existing BMSs. To address this issue, we propose a set of basic and generic components of BMSs, as well as how these components can be flexibly modelled to satisfy different booking contexts. Such components include resources, bookings, booking constraints, booking workflows, time. We believe that the consideration of these components by developers can lead to implementation of reusable BMSs for organizations whose requirements are not yet satisfied in existing BMSs.

Keywords: Resource booking · Resource scheduling · Reservation

1 Introduction

Booking, which is the act of reserving resources in advance, is an important component of planning-related activities [1]. These activities vary from simple activities involving the maintenance of personal schedules to the much more complex inventory and supply chain management in Enterprise Resource Planning activities. In some organizations e.g., airlines, hotels, rental services (cars, video, sport facilities, etc. rentals), logistics companies, resource booking constitutes a critical component of the business model.

Typically, bookings are managed by a Bookings Management System (BMS), which aims at controlling the access of people to scarce resources at a specified future time interval. Lately, online BMS are increasingly being adopted by organizations and used by people due to their easiness, efficiency, availability and cost effectiveness [2]. Due to the pervasive nature of booking related activities, several BMSs have emerged. However, a common issue with existing BMSs is that they are typically designed to meet the requirements of *some* specific context. Such a context may be a specific scenario or use case of an organization or professional discipline. Consequently, there exist many BMSs, all of which have similar functionality which are inflexible and not reusable

© Springer International Publishing Switzerland 2016
M. Felderer et al. (Eds.): ERP Future 2015 - Research, LNBIP 245, pp. 73–80, 2016.
DOI: 10.1007/978-3-319-32799-0_6

outside the exact context for which they were developed. For instance, a typical room-booking BMS is not reusable for laboratory equipment booking, although their basic functionality needed is relatively the same. This large diversity of related, yet not easily reusable BMSs can be attributed to the following reasons:

- Inflexible modelling of resources, booking period, booking constraints etc. For instance, a "car" BMS may not be re-usable as a "playground" BMS because its resource type is rigidly set to cars in the application. Similarly, some BMSs assume that the booking time granularity is in hours, while others assume days.
- Some BMSs are not reused in some contexts because they do not provide the necessary booking functionalities required within those other booking contexts.
- A lot of the non-booking related functionalities in some BMSs can modify the core booking functionality to an extent that makes it un-reusable in contexts other than the one for which it was originally designed. For instance, a library BMS may have several other institution-specific components to which it is tightly coupled, and which influences how the BMS is designed.

As a result, there is usually the duplication of BMS development efforts across organizations even if the differences in booking requirements are minor. Although, existing BMSs can satisfy a large number of booking requirements, they cannot satisfy all foreseeable requirements in all booking contexts. Hence, to address the reusability issue, we believe there is a need to identify a set of core components of BMSs, and model them in a way such that they can be easily and flexibly re-used in different booking contexts. To satisfy this objective, we believe BMSs need to be designed to be

- Generic i.e. independent of any specific booking context
- Configurable to satisfy the simple requirements of the several booking contexts, without the need for any additional software development task.
- Extendable with additional functionality to address complex context specific requirements

The fundamental purpose of this paper, therefore, is to identify and compile the set of key components of a generic BMS, together with inter-relationship of these compiled set of components. To the best of our knowledge, there has not been really strong research effort along the direction of building such a generic BMS. Our aim is not to specify implementation decisions or procedure. Instead, it is more about what should be considered in the implementation of generic BMS and leaves the "how to do it" to the implementers.

The remainder of this paper is organized as follows- in Sect. 2, we present our motivation as well as the requirements we used in compiling the components of our proposed BMS. In Sect. 3, we review related works, and in Sect. 4, we highlight the components of proposed BMS. The implementation of the BMS is discussed in Sect. 5 and in Sect. 6, we present the conclusion.

2 Motivation and Requirements

Our work was initially motivated by the need of some research projects to have a generic platform for managing the access to the resources used for data collection. One of such projects is the Biodiversity Exploratories (BE) – a research project which studies relationship between land use, ecosystem processes and biodiversity in different areas in Germany. Example of the type of resources managed within this project includes plot areas, bedrooms, beds, experiments, laboratory, cars, nets, ploughs, binoculars, laboratory refrigerators, books, and several other data collection equipment. Some of these resources have constraints (e.g. resource dependencies) that needs to be satisfied at booking time, while some others have a set of booking steps (workflow) that should be followed before their booking is approved. Similarly, different types of resources have different properties (e.g. resource "car" can have "brand name" property, while resource "plot" may have "location" property), and these resources should be discoverable based on their properties. In addition, different resources can have different booking time granularity i.e. the minimum period for which they can be booked. For example, some resources are bookable on daily basis, while some other resources are bookable on hourly basis. Furthermore, the functionalities of the BMS exposed to a system user (e.g. creating or deleting a resource, making a booking, approving a booking, viewing the resource booking schedule) should also be based on the rights of the user in the system. Another key requirement of the BE project is that all these resources should be managed within a single application framework, irrespective of the resource's peculiarities. Other requirements relates to the resource allocation algorithm (i.e. how booking approval decision is made) specification, booking event (set of booking made for a purpose) management, etc.

Based on the above requirements as well as the requirements collected in the review of related works (see Sect. 3), we recognize that the over-arching requirement of a generic BMS the flexibility of the application with respect to the definition and usage of the basic BMS components (e.g. resource, booking, booking workflow, time, booking constraints).

3 Related Works

Several BMSs are developed to satisfy the requirements of the specific context in which they are developed. In this section, we review relevant BMSs with respect to the different booking requirements they try to satisfy, and how they address the problem of reusability.

According to [4], BMS should be able to store, publish and update the dynamic resource availability and prices, and additionally provide the users with a regular reservation process. In [5], 21 hotel reservation management systems are compared based on functional and usability based booking requirements in the hotel industry. Such requirements include booking handling, price control, payment handling, website design, user friendliness etc. Similarly, [6] evaluated 10 restaurant table reservation systems based on 25 criteria including ease of use, price management, auto confirmation of booking, statistics reporting functionally, personalization functionality, picture upload functionality etc. Likewise, [7] compared around 50 class/course booking systems based on functionalities such as event scheduling, course management and editing, and examination registration functionality. Furthermore, [8] reviewed different systems for booking remote laboratories, e.g., WebLab, NetLab, LiLa, iLab, with respect to functionalities such as ticketing, accommodation management, tours and events, group check-in, reporting etc.

Furthermore, the functional requirements of BMSs for some specific use cases have been highlighted in some papers. Some of these functional requirements vary from very detailed, to broach over-arching, to abstract specifications. For a staff appointment scheduling system, functionalities for reporting, security, reminders, access are required according to [1]. In [9], requirements such as management of user, reservations, dynamic pricing, inventory, availability, personalization etc., are specified for a hotel reservation application. Similarly, [10] specified functionalities for managing user access, consultation with lecturers, appointment, calendar module, report module in a web-based appointment management system.

Overall, the reviewed BMSs are developed to satisfy the requirements based in some given contexts. However, they all share the basic functionality of reserving access to resources at a future time based on business rules, workflow or algorithms.

To address the problem of interoperability and re-usability of reservation systems, [11] opined that such system needs to be modular. Hence, [12, 13] proposed the use of service oriented architecture (SOA). The main functionalities provided in [12] include user, resource and reservation administration, while [13] focus on providing functionalities for planning, searching and reserving resources. However, other functionalities such as constraints, booking workflow etc. are needed in order to have a minimally useful BMS. Besides, setting up such a SOA-based systems is complex.

[12, 14] highlight a generic resource booking process that contains components such as resource time and capacity querying, resource offering, resource selection, resource reservation, resource acceptance and resource booking. Similarly, [14] highlight the modules in generic BMS architecture. This includes modules for reservation management, resource characteristics management, notification component, user management, and announcement system.

4   Components of the Proposed BMS

An overview of the major components of our proposed BMS is shown in Fig. 1. These are presented as a model based on using the UML specification. Each of our proposed component is represented as a UML package (which is used to group classes, objects, elements, etc. used in providing a particular functionality).

One of the central concepts in our model is the *Resource* package which is used for creating, managing, and discovery of resources. Information such as quantity of resources, booking granularity of a resource, grouping of resources are managed here as well.

The *Resource* package relies on the *Resource Structure* package to define the structure and organization of the set of attributes of a set of resources in the *Resource* package. To a certain extent, the *Resource Structure* can be viewed as the schema definition package for the set of resources in the *Resource* package. Different *Resource Structures* (schemas) can be defined for different types of resources and managed within the same application framework. Every resource created in the *Resource* package is based on a structure which is defined in the *Resource Structure* package. In order to facilitate discovery, *Resource Structures* share attributes (e.g. "car" and "room" resource structure can share attribute "color"). They also be able to inherit from one another e.g. a "classroom" resource structure can inherit from a "room" resource structure. These functionalities for managing the above described inheritance and sharing of attributes are managed in the *Resource Structure* package as well.

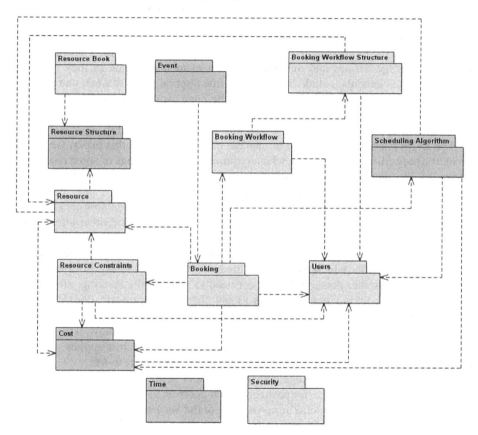

Fig. 1. Overview of the major components of the proposed RBM

The *Resource Book* package is the container for different resource structures, as well as the different types of information which is provided to, and shared within the BMS application. Such information may include news, information about the resource book or some particular resource etc.

The set of constraints associated with booking a resource is managed in the *Resource Constraints* package. The constraints are specified for the booking of some resources at a particular period of time for some specific users. Constraints managed in the *Resource Constraints* package can specify dependency between resources (i.e. which resources should be booked with other resources), restriction on the reservation of some users at a time, or the restriction on the quantity of a resource a user is allowed to book.

Based on the set of constraints on the resources, the booking of the resources is done in the *Booking* package which manages the reservation of a resource to a user. The booking process is also dependent on the *Scheduling Algorithm* package, which should specify how to allocate the resources to satisfy the aim of the BMS providers (the organization who is managing the resource booking using the BMS). The "first come, first served" algorithm is typically used in many system.

Booking associates a resource (managed in the *Resource* package) to some person (managed using the *Users* package) for a period of time (managed in the *Time* package). The time package defines and manages different elements of time as they relate to booking. These elements include time instant, time interval, units of time, unit conversion functionality, periodic time interval, etc. The *Time* package is also associated with other packages such as *Resource Constraints, Events, Booking Workflow,* and *Cost.* However, for the sake of clarity, the association is not depicted in Fig. 1.

The *Event* package can be used to manage booking event. In this paper, we define event as a happening or occurrence which requires a set of bookings of some resources. Therefore, the event can be considered as a container for a set of bookings that were jointly made together for some specific tasks.

Similarly, associated with the *Booking* package is a *Booking Workflow* package, and this manages the process of booking, the status of booking, as well as other information associated with every booking status. In order to understand a booking workflow, consider the use case where a user who wants to book a car need to first register his interest in the car, after which the status of the booking changes to say "user has registered interest". Another personnel may later need to approve the booking, after which the status of the booking status changes to say "booking approved". This described sample workflow can be defined and managed in the *Booking Workflow Structure* package which is used to define the structure of the booking workflow. The booking workflow structure is also associated with the resource to which it applies, and it is instantiated into a resource workflow during the booking of the resource.

Furthermore, the *Users* package manages the users of the system. Tightly linked to the *Users* package is the *Security* package which controls the users' access and rights to the components of the model. The association of the *Security* package to all the other packages of our model is not shown in the diagram for the sake of clarity.

The *Cost* package provides the functionality for modeling and managing costs (financial or otherwise) associated with resources and bookings at a particular time.

5 Implementation and Deployment

As a first use-case, we have a prototype implementation of the core components of this BMS model which will be used for the resource booking in the Biodiversity Exploratories project (introduced in Sect. 1). There is an existing BMS application in this project, which is inflexible, and not easily reusable, and this has been used for the project's resource booking management since 2007. Data collected in this existing project's BMS system is currently being used to test the compliance of our system with the BMS requirements specified in Sect. 2.

We plan to provide our implementation of this BMS components as an independent web application, and as a software library. This implementation work is done within the context of the development of a research data management application called BExIS 2 (details available in [15]). This BMS application will be made available within this framework under a GNU Lesser General Public License version 3.

6 Conclusion

Several BMSs have been developed for managing access to resources at a future time interval; however, many of them have been modelled and developed to tightly fit the requirements of some specific contexts (use cases). This can lead to lack of reusability and duplication of modelling and development efforts as existing BMSs cannot satisfy all foreseeable booking requirements in all booking contexts. To address this issue, we compiled a list of the basic component of a generic BMS together with their associations. These components include resource, booking, booking workflow, booking time period, booking workflow, booking constraints.

For managing the configurability and flexibility of the basic BMS components for different booking contexts, we also proposed other components such as the resource structure, and the booking workflow structure component.

Furthermore, an application has been developed based on this model within the BExIS 2 application framework, and it is being tested with booking data collected from an existing BMS application used in the Biodiversity Exploratories project.

The objective of this paper is not to find one-size-fits-all BMS solution. Instead, it is more about what should be considered in the implementation of generic BMS and leaves the "how to do it" to the implementers.

Acknowledgments. We would like to thank the members of the Biodiversity Exploratories for making their data available via our data repository, BExIS.

Further, we thank Christiane Fischer giving support through the central office, the Local Management Team, and Markus Fischer, Eduard Linsenmair, Dominik Hessenmöller, Jens Nieschulze, Daniel Prati, Ingo Schöning, François Buscot, Ernst-Detlef Schulze, Wolfgang W. Weisser and the late Elisabeth Kalko for their role in setting up the Biodiversity Exploratories project. Among these, special thanks are due to Jens Nieschulze and Ernst-Detlef Schulze for initiating and developing BExIS for the first years of the Exploratories. The work has been (partly) funded by the DFG Priority Program 1374 "Infrastructure-Biodiversity-Exploratories" (BR 2315/7-2).

References

1. Coley, C.T., Nessland, K.S., Leonhardt, T.F., Barry, C.J., Wilson, M.F., Nettuno, A.N.: Systems and methods for on-line scheduling of appointments and other resources. US Patent 8,671,009 (2014)
2. CWT Travel Management Institute: Business Traveler Services - Finding the right fit (2011). http://www.carlsonwagonlit.com/export/sites/cwt/en/global/insights/travel-management-institute/pdf/lever1_en.pdf. Accessed on 15 August 2015
3. AppointmentPlus: Manual vs automated appointment scheduling (2012). https://www.appointment-plus.com/pdf/resources/manual_vs_automated_appointment_scheduling.pdf. Accessed on 15 August 2015
4. Landvogt, M.: Online booking engines for small and medium-sized enterprises as a tool for improved distribution and yield management in New Zealand's tourism industry. In: Proceedings of New Zealand Tourism and Hospitality Conference, pp. 191–198 (2004)
5. Ivanov, S.: Conceptual marketing framework for online hotel reservation system design. Tourism Today 8(2008), 7–32 (2008). doi:10.2139/ssrn.1296040
6. Anderegg, D., Zhang, X., Berger, T, Malicovscaia, I.: Evaluation of Table Reservation Systems for Restaurants, Lucerne School of Business (2014). https://www.gastroprofessional.ch/dbFile/295694/Evaluation_of_Table_Reservation.pdf. Accessed on 15 August 2015
7. Kraigher P.: High Level Assessment Scheduling Software, Report for the University of British Columbia (2010). http://www.students.ubc.ca/mura/tasks/sites/classroomservices/cache/file/07B84FD2-C29E-CEA0-7CA6BFA8E80E9F4D.pdf. Accessed on 15 August 2015
8. Maiti, A., Maxwell, A.D., Kist, A.A.: An overview of system architectures for remote laboratories. In: TALE, pp. 26–29 (2013). doi:10.1109/TALE.2013.6654520
9. Singh, A., Kamath, R.: An integrated property & guest management system, Infosys White Paper (2013). http://www.infosys.com/industries/hospitality-leisure/white-papers/Documents/guest-management-system.pdf
10. Lu, K.M., Hamid, S.T.A.: Conceptual Design of Web-Based Appointment Management System using Object WebML. Information Technologies and Applications in Education (ISITAE'07). IEEE Conference Proceeding, pp. 354–359 (2007)
11. Leach, R.L.: Software Reuse: Methods, Models, and Costs. McGraw-Hill, New York (1997)
12. Dorn, J., Werthner, H.: Service-oriented resource management. In: Proceedings of the 41st Annual Hawaii International Conference on System Sciences (2008)
13. Zhou, F., Chusho, T.: A web application framework for reservation systems and its reusability evaluation. In: Proceedings of the 2009 IAENG International Conference on Software Engineering (ICSE 2009), pp. 1027–1032, March 2009
14. Wolf, L.C., Steinmetz, R.: Concepts for reservation in advance. Kluwer J. Multimedia Tools Appl. 4(3) (1997)
15. Chamanara, J., König-Ries, B.: A conceptual model for data management in the field of ecology. Ecol. Inform. (2013). doi:10.1016/j.ecoinf.2013.12.003

Strategic Management in the Branch of Online Accounting Solution Providers

Sandra-Lorena Bahlmann[1](✉) and Felix Piazolo[2]

[1] University of Innsbruck, Innsbruck, Austria
Sandra-Lorena.Bahlmann@uibk.ac.at
[2] Andrassy University Budapest, Budapest, Hungary
felix.piazolo@andrassyuni.hu

Abstract. The purpose of this study is to figure out to what extent organizations are implementing the concept of strategic management. The research focus is on the cloud based online accounting market. The importance of this study derives, because there is a positive correlation between the application of strategic management and economical success. As a fundamental model, the approach of strategic management by Hans H. Hinterhuber will be used. To explore the degree of implementation a qualitative content analysis was carried out. Furthermore a tool for evaluation of the implementation was elaborated. The dimension product strategy was added to the underlying approach. Important insights regarding the implementation and the differences between start-ups and longer established organizations derived. The result of this study is that the strategic management is implemented to a mediocre degree. Furthermore, the study shows where the deficits according to the implementation lie.

Keywords: Strategic management · Enterprise systems · Online accounting · Cloud computing · Start ups

1 Introduction

Cloud computing is one of the upcoming trends in the world of Information Technology (IT) and the industry [1]. The popularity on this topic increases among organizations and consumers. Therefore, there is no doubt that the hype about the cloud computing trend will continue [2].

Characterizing for the cloud business are cost benefits and the easy usage [3, 4]. Thus, it is not surprising that software companies in the German, Austrian and Swiss market offer and use cloud-based products. In 2009, 10 % of the organizations operating in Germany, Austria and Switzerland counted cloud computing to their IT-Strategy [5]. Nowadays companies operating in Germany, Austria and Switzerland get 28.60 % percent of all their IT services from the cloud [6]. According to Gartner cloud computing is getting part of the mainstream adaption very soon [7].

In the German, Austrian and Swiss market of online accounting products the number of organizations offering products in the cloud is increasing. While some organizations still hold on to on premise solutions, others have already recognized the potential of the

© Springer International Publishing Switzerland 2016
M. Felderer et al. (Eds.): ERP Future 2015 - Research, LNBIP 245, pp. 81–94, 2016.
DOI: 10.1007/978-3-319-32799-0_7

cloud business and its benefits. Innovations arise and new competitors still enter. Characterizing for this market is that start-ups and longer established organizations compete against each other.

Especially the diversity of companies and the dynamic market conditions make the exploration of strategies crucial. It is of high interest, if organizations with unequal organizational structures implement the strategic management in a different way. There is to find out, whether there is a difference in the application of strategic management for start-ups and longer established organizations. Furthermore, the existence or non-existence of differences in the implementation of the different components of strategic management is essential for further studies. In general, the implementation of a sustainable strategy process is very important for all type of organizations [8]. Therefore it is more likely that an organization that follows a good strategy is continuously successful [9]. Different studies even confirm a positive correlation between the application of strategic management and economical success [10–12]. Start-ups and longer established organizations have in common that one of their main goals is to gain economical success for their survival. From this connection results the importance of a study that evaluates the implementation of strategic management in the branch of online accounting software.

A substantial part of the published work on the topic business software deals with implementation and post implementation issues of ERP software systems and the purchase and buying process of IT [13–16]. Literature on online accounting software in the cloud lacks so far. Research that links strategic management with the online accounting market is for the most parts being ignored.

The aim of this work is to deliver an insight into the implementation of strategic management of organizations operating in the cloud based online accounting market. The work highlights the implementation of the different components of the strategic management concept. Furthermore it determines the degree of operationalization of the different strategic management components. It indicates if there are differences in the implementation of strategic management between start-ups and longer established organizations.

2   Theoretical Background: Strategic Management and the Online Accounting Market

Online accounting software is dealing with all kind of accounting transactions. Examples are trial balance, accounts payable, accounts receivable, general ledger or payroll [17]. It is continuously developed and extended. Add-ons as well as interfaces to other programs are additional offers. Online accounting software is a type of Enterprise Application (EA)-Software. Cloud based online accounting software has all the advantages of an on premise online accounting solution and combines it with the advantages of cloud computing.

In the German, Austrian and Swiss market, 69.56 % (16 out of 23) of the organizations offer modular online accounting solutions to their consumers. In contrast, 39.13 % (9 out of 23) offer their cloud based online accounting product as part of an integrated overall solution. Two organizations offer both. Integrated overall solutions include other business application software solutions in order to offer the complete package that is necessary to run a business. Modular solutions are specified on just one or a few business application software modules (Fig. 1).

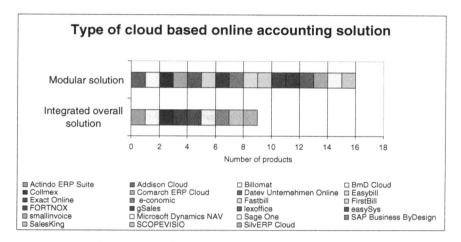

Fig. 1. Type of cloud based online accounting solutions [18]

There are two types of online accounting software products. One is developed for the usage of organizations and the other one for the usage of tax advisors. As you can see in Fig. 2, most of the companies in this market develop and offer software for organizations. Additionally the target market can be separated into company sizes. Most of the products offered in the Online Accounting market are produced for small enterprises or self-employed entrepreneurs. Only two of the products serve large enterprises and 13 of 23 products are satisfying the needs of the medium-sized enterprises. Generally, the software solutions are produced for more than one target group. Mostly, solutions for quotation/order/invoice, customer relationship management (CRM) or for enterprise resource planning (ERP) are offered together within the accounting module. In contrast, modules for payroll & salary accounting or production are exceptional. In most cases they are not offered together with the accounting solution [18].

Characterising for the German, Austrian and Swiss market is that it is relatively young. There are still organizations entering the market [19]. As mentioned, most of the organizations are specialized on fulfilling the requirements of one or two of the mentioned target groups. Another differentiation between the organizations offering online accounting products is, that some base the development of their cloud software on their before existing on premise solution. In contrast, Start-ups develop the software without any basis solution. Therefore it is crucial to find out if there are any differences in the implementation of strategic management of start-ups and longer established organizations.

Generally, the strategic management concept focuses on all activities, as i.e. development, planning and implementation of a market-based organization. It involves the

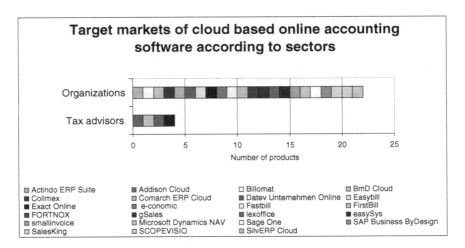

Fig. 2. Target markets of cloud based online accounting software [18]

internal organization as well as the external stakeholders. Thereby it enables a holistic view of the organization. In this study, the strategic management approach by Hinterhuber is used as basic concept. It is discussed in theory and tested in the practice [20, 21].

The strategic management approach by Hinterhuber explains the interrelationships of the different components of an organization [9]. It describes how to manage them to satisfy the strategic stakeholders. The approach consists of eight dimensions - corporate vision, corporate politics and goals, strategies, action plans, structure and processes, implementation, corporate culture and identity and strategic controlling – which are influenced by the leaders to a holistic concept [9]. Gaining a holistic view of the organization is very important. It enables the leaders to understand how the different components relate to each other and how the decisions which have been made in the different parts of the organization influence each other. The aim of this approach is to harmonize the different components to an overall strategic concept. Furthermore it should be developed and adapted continuously to the changing external environment. A continuous learning process works as a basis for this integrated management concept. Core task of this stakeholder orientated approach is to gain sustainable long-term success. Hitt et al. also mention the importance of the focus on sustainability [8]. As already mentioned, different studies confirm a positive correlation between the application of strategic management and economical success [10–12]. In how far organizations in the cloud based online accounting market implement the different components of strategic management, will be examined in this study (Fig. 3).

Most of the organizations in the respective market are one-product companies. As this kind of companies focus on just one product instead of a wider product portfolio, it can be assumed that the importance of the product strategy increases. Therefore, this study includes the component product strategy into the model of Hinterhuber. This makes it possible to examine the importance of the product strategy in the respective market. For organizations offering a bundle of products, their cloud based online accounting product was considered in this study. As in the software industry one-product

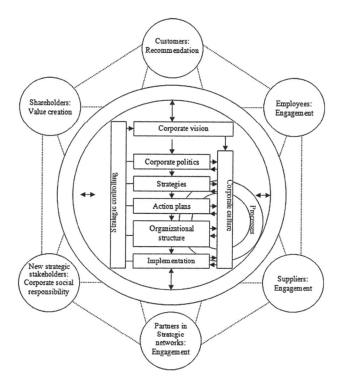

Fig. 3. Strategic management approach by Hinterhuber [9]

companies are very common, the results of this study are of high interest for the whole industry [22].

3 Empirical Study on the Strategic Management in the Cloud Based Online Accounting Market

A qualitative study is conducted. It examines how far the different components of the strategic management concept by Hinterhuber are implemented. Insofar the online accounting market is reviewed for its orientation towards sustainable long-term success. The study concentrates on the implementation of the internal components of strategic management that are relevant for success. In contrast to the outer components, they can be directly influenced by the leaders. The outer part that contains the strategic stakeholders is not considered in this study. The product strategy is added to the approach (Fig. 4).

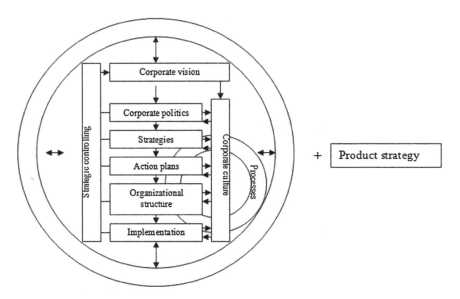

Fig. 4. Components of strategic management examined in the online accounting market [9]

23 organizations representing the online accounting market were asked to participate in this study, partly orally on the CEBIT exhibition centre in Hannover and inn some cases via email. The selection was based on predetermined criteria. Their belonging to the German, Austrian and Swiss market and to the cloud based online accounting market were the criteria for the selection. Additionally the position of the interview partner as a senior executive and his expert knowledge on the theme were crucial for the selection as a interview partner. The guideline based interviews contained 22 questions, 2 questions for each component of the strategic management approach. The questions are partly based on the questionnaire of a quantitative study by Piazolo et al. on implementation of strategic management in franchise systems [23]. All of the questions align with the strategic management concept by Hinterhuber [9].

7 out of 23 organizations took part at the interview. This represents a response rate of 30.43 %. Five of them where conducted orally on the 16/03/2015 and the 17/3/2015 at the CeBIT trade exhibition in Hannover. Additionally, two interviews were held out via Skype and telephone on the 27/04/2015 and the 12/05/2015. The interviews were mainly recorded digitally and then transcribed. Two interviews where logged due to the rejection of the interview recording by two parties.

Subsequently, the transcripts were evaluated according to the qualitative content analysis method by Mayring [24]. Similar to the questions from the guideline the relevant passages were paraphrased. Afterwards 514 different ID-Items were coded and 11 categories where formed deductively with respect to the underlying theory. Only the explicit responses of the interviewees have been taken into account.

The categories were additionally divided into 22 sub-categories, which are based on the questions asked. Therefore, every sub-dimension of the strategic management approach by Hinterhuber is equivalent to a sub-category that was deductively formed.

Each category consists of two sub-categories. The deductively formed categories correspond to the dimensions of strategic management (Fig. 5).

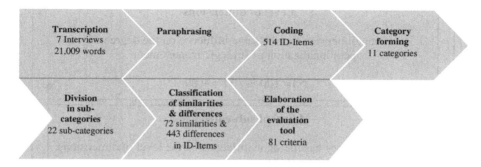

Fig. 5. Methodology

Then, the ID-Items were classified by similarities and differences. In 72 cases, two or more companies acted the same way. In 443 cases, the behavior of the organizations was different.

Hereafter, the evaluation tool for the implementation of strategic management according to Hinterhuber was elaborated. The evaluation tool consists of a criteria list for each sub-category. The criteria are based on the approach by Hinterhuber. When applying the evaluation tool it was reviewed, if the ID-Items confirm with the different criteria. To which degree the organizations implement the concept of strategic management was evaluated in this study (Fig. 6).

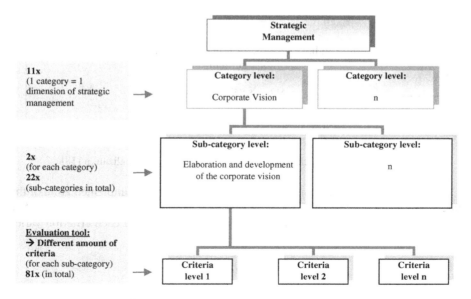

Fig. 6. Categories, sub-categories and criteria

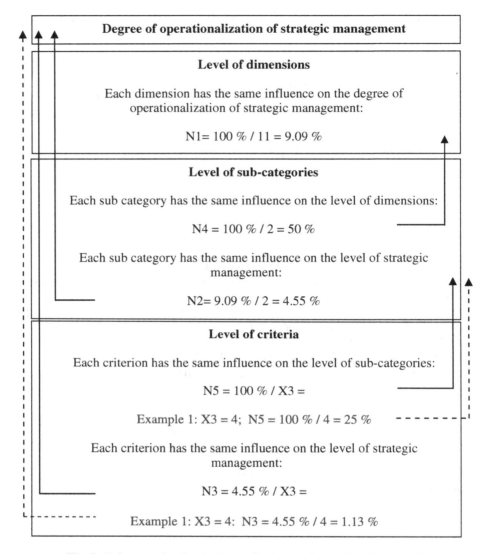

Fig. 7. Influence of each criterion on the degree of operationalization [18]

Each dimension has an influence of 9.09 % on the degree of implementation of the strategic management concept. The different sub-categories have an influence of 4.55 % on the overall degree of strategic management. The influence of each criterion varies according to the number of criteria in one sub-category.

4   Findings: Degree of Operationalization of Strategic Management

The degree of operationalization of the different dimensions of the strategic management concept is composed of the means of the two sub-categories of each dimension. For the overall degree of the strategic management the dimensions are rated equally. The degree of operationalization is presented on a scale of 0 - 100 %. Fulfilling 100 % means a full operationalization of strategic management. On the other hand, 0 % means that the operationalization of strategic management is not considered according to the approach of Hinterhuber (Fig. 7).

Generally companies in the industry of online accounting software in the cloud apply the elements of strategic management to a mediocre degree of 68.30 %. But there are still big differences between the different elements. As you can see in Fig. 8, the elements product strategy, strategic controlling, corporate strategy and organization on average score well and have a degree of operationalization of at least 75 %. The product strategy is operationalized higher that the other dimensions with a degree of 92.86 %. Therefore, it can be assumed, that the organizations in the online accounting market find this dimension to be very important. In opposition the elements processes and plans for action score low. The value of these components is below 50 % and points out the deficiencies in the application of the strategic management approach for organizations offering online accounting products in the cloud.

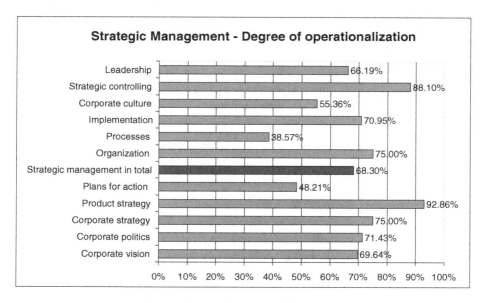

Fig. 8.   Degree of operationalization [18]

The degree of operationalization of strategic management of the different companies varies between 57,84 % and 84,85 % as you can see in Fig. 9. The organizations A to F have a degree of operationalization of up to 70 % and just organization G scores high with a degree of 84,85 %. Especially organization D with a degree of 57,84 % has high

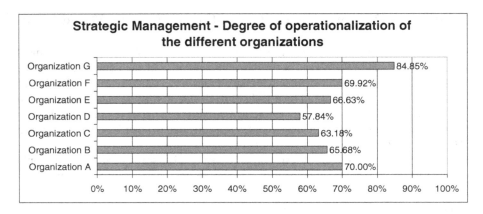

Fig. 9. Degree of operationalization of the different organizations [18]

deficiencies in the implementation of the strategic management approach, as well as organization C with a degree of 63,18 %.

The start-ups in this group, Organizations A and F, operationalize the strategic management approach to a degree of 69.92 % and 70 %. Most of the longer established organizations operationalize the strategic management to a lower degree. Just organization G stands out. It operationalizes the strategic management to a degree of 84,85 %. There is no significant difference in the application of strategic management between start-ups and longer established organizations and no trend into one direction.

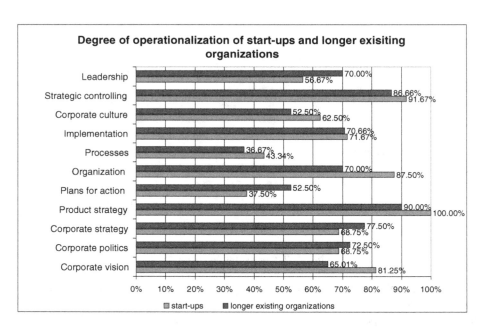

Fig. 10. Degree of operationalization of start-ups and longer established organizations

When considering the different components of strategic management high differences between start-ups and longer established organizations occur in the elements leadership, corporate culture, organization, plans for action, product strategy and corporate vision. As you can see in Fig. 10, the degree of operationalization varies about 10 % or more. The components implementation and corporate politics are operationalized to a similar degree in start-ups and longer established organizations. Longer established organizations have their focus on the product strategy, strategic controlling and the corporate strategy. Start-ups focus on the product strategy, strategic controlling, organization and the corporate vision.

When explicitly considering the two start-ups in this study it is outstanding that the individual companies vary significantly in their application of the different components. As you can see in Fig. 11, just in the components processes (43,34 %) and the product strategy (100 %) a consistent application can be seen.

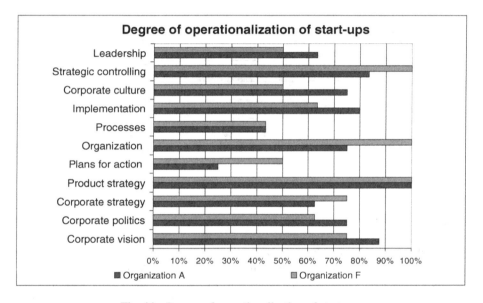

Fig. 11. Degree of operationalization of start-ups

For longer established organizations a consistent application can be seen in the component product strategy and corporate strategy. For the other components of strategic management the application varies significantly according to the individual companies. Therefore, each organization implements strategic management components in a different way. There is no consistent pattern for the implementation (Fig. 12).

Therefore it is not proven, that start-ups and longer established organizations implement the different components of strategic management significantly different. Start-ups and longer established organizations don't follow a special trend.

Fig. 12. Degree of operationalization of longer established organizations

5   Conclusion

Based on the data evaluation the organizations operating in the online accounting market apply the elements of strategic management to a mediocre degree. Their orientation towards sustainable long-term success is still extendable. The components product strategy, strategic controlling, corporate strategy and organization are implemented to a high degree. The product strategy is operationalized higher than all the other elements. Therefore, it can be assumed, that the organizations in the online accounting market find this dimension to be very important. Deficits are in the elements processes, plans for action and corporate culture. The implementation doesn't differ significantly for start-ups and longer established organizations.

5.1   Theoretical Implications and Limitations of the Study

The study shows that the method regarding the evaluation of the implementation of the elements of strategic management is appropriate. The degree of operationalization and furthermore deep insights into the extent of the implementation could be detected. A comparative study should confirm this. However, only two subcategories of each dimension were considered. Therefore it is recommended to conduct a more comprehensive study that considers further sub-dimensions. Additionally the study should be extended to other industries. A further implication is to elaborate a uniform evaluation tool. This study is based on a qualitative research, while a study on the implementation of strategic management for franchise systems [23] is based on a quantitative research. A uniform evaluation tool would make the results of different studies comparable. As the product strategy has been operationalized to a high degree, the appearance as own dimension in the market online accounting has proven to be right. It seems to be of high importance for this market. Nonetheless, an additional study should confirm the appearance of the product strategy as an own dimension by considering it more in detail.

5.2 Managerial Implications

As already mentioned, the deficits are in the dimensions processes, plans for action and corporate culture, as they score lowest. The managerial implications result from analyzing the evaluation tool.

In the dimension processes the management should consider process optimization as a clear goal of the executive board. Furthermore, the top management should implement a process owner. Additionally, the elaboration of a success-orientated controlling and incentive system helps to obtain process optimization.

An implication for the top-management in the component plans for action is to encourage the heads of functional areas and the managers to work together on the plans for action. The responsibility of the plans for action is meant to be on the managers who have elaborated them.

Furthermore, the top management can align their corporate culture to the strategic management approach by sharing stories and myths about key figures. The elaboration of a leadership mission statement is recommended for the organizations lacking one. Additionally the top management should communicate the mission statement of the organization during job interviews.

The question if the online accounting market stands out positively from other branches according to its implementation of strategic management remains unanswered.

References

1. Jiang, J., Yang, G.: Examining cloud computing from the perspective of grid and computer-supported cooperative work. In: Antonopoulos, N., Gillam, L. (eds.) Cloud Computing: Principles, Systems and Applications, pp. 63–76. Springer, London (2010)
2. International Data Corporation: Forecast of Public IT Cloud services. http://www.idc.com/getdoc.jsp?containerId=prUS25219014
3. Mell, P., Grance, T.: The NIST Definition of Cloud Computing: Recommendations of the National Institute of Standards and Technology, NIST Special Publication 800–145. http://csrc.nist.gov/publications/nistpubs/800-145/SP800-145.pdf
4. Szer, B.: Cloud Computing und Wissensmanagement: Bewertung von Wissensmanagementsystemen in der Cloud. Diplomica Verlag, Hamburg (2013)

5. Jendrosch, T., Pohl, E., Zwick, M., Zwick, V.E.: Berufs- und Karriere-Planer: IT und Wirtschaft 2010/2011, 11th edn. Gabler Springer Fachmedien Verlag, Wiesbaden (2011). pp. 20–26
6. Capgemini: Study IT-Trends (2015). https://www.at.capgemini.com/resource-file-access/resource/pdf/it-trends-studie-2015.pdf
7. Gartner: Hype Cycle for Emerging Techonogies (2014). http://www.gartner.com/newsroom/id/2819918
8. Hitt, M.A., Ireland, R.D., Hoskisson, R.E.: Strategic Management: Competitiveness and Globalisation: Concept and Cases, 11th edn. South-Western College Pub, Cincinnati (2014)
9. Hinterhuber, H.H.: Strategische Unternehmensführung: Das Gesamtmodell für nachhaltige Wertsteigerung, 9th edn. Erich Schmidt Verlag, Berlin (2015)
10. Michel, R.: Know-how der Unternehmensplanung: Budgetierung, Controlling, takt. Planung, Langfristplanung und Strategie. Sauer-Verlag, Heidelberg (1986)
11. Covin, J.G., Slevin, D.P.: Strategic management of small firms in hostile and benign environments. Strateg. Manag. J. 10(1), 75–87 (1989)
12. Rhyne, J.L., Lawrence, C.: The relationship of strategic planning to financial performance. Strateg. Manag. J. 7(5), 423–436 (1986)
13. Esteves, J., Pastor, J.: Enterprise resource planning systems research: an annotated bibliography. Commun. AIS 7(8), 1–52 (2001)
14. Verville, J.C.: An empirical study of organizational buying behavior: a critical investigation of the acquisition of ERP software. Dissertation, Université Laval, Québec (2000)
15. Geisler, E., Hoang, W.: Purchasing information technologies: behaviour patterns of service companies. Int. J. Purchasing Mater. Manag. 28(3), 38–42 (1992)
16. Verville, J., Halingten, A.: A six-stage model of the buying process for ERP software. Ind. Mark. Manag. 32(7), 585–594 (2003)
17. Davenport, T.H.: Putting the enterprise into the enterprise system. Harvard Bus. Rev. 76(4), 121–131 July–August (1998).
18. Bahlmann, S.-L.: Strategic management in the branch of online accounting solution providers. Master thesis, Universität Innsbruck, Innsbruck (2015)
19. ADDISON: ADDISON OneClick. http://www.addison.de/ueber-addison/aktuelles/detail/mitteilung/addison-oneclick-ist-online.html
20. Hahn, D., Taylor, B.: Strategische Unternehmungsplanung: Stand und Entwicklungstendenzen, 5th edn. Physica-Verlag HD, Heidelberg (1990)
21. Hinterhuber, H.H., Friedrich, S.A., Matzler, K., Stahl, H.K.: Die rolle der kundenzufriedenheit in der strategischen unternehmensführung. In: Hinterhuber, H.H., Matzler, K. (eds.) Kundenorientierte Unternehmensführung: Kundenorientierung, Kundenzufriedenheit, Kundenbindung, pp. 3–22. Gabler Verlag, Wiesbaden (2000)
22. Bretschneider, U., Ebner, W., Leimeister, J.M., Krcmar, H.: Internetbasierte Ideenwettbewerbe als Instrument der Integration von Kunden in das Innovationsmanagement von Software-Unternehmen. Conference paper, Gemeinschaften in neuen Medien (GeNeMe), Dresden (2007)
23. Piazolo, F., Hinterhuber, H.H., Promberger, K.: Strategische führung in franchisesystemen: eine empirische untersuchung im deutschsprachigen raum. In: Kaltenbrunner, K.A., Urnik, S. (eds.) Unternehmensführung: State of the art und Entwicklungsperspektiven, pp. 195–212. Oldenbourg Verlag, München (2012)
24. Mayring, P.: Qualitative Inhaltsanalyse: Grundlagen und Techniken, 12th edn. Beltz Pädagogik, Weinheim (2015)

The Austrian ERP Market: Systems in Use, System Vendors and Implementation Consultancies

Lukas Paa[1,2]([⊠]), Felix Piazolo[1,2], and Christoph Weiss[1,2]

[1] Andrássy University Budapest, Pollack Mihály Tér 3, 1088 Budapest, Hungary
{lukas.paa, felix.piazolo,
christoph.weiss}@andrassyuni.hu
[2] Department of Strategic Management, Marketing and Tourism,
University of Innsbruck, Universitätsstraße 15, 6020 Innsbruck, Austria
{lukas.paa, felix.piazolo, christoph.weiss}@uibk.ac.at
http://www.andrassyuni.hu
http://www.uibk.ac.at/smt

Abstract. This paper summarizes the results of a quantitative survey on the Austrian market of enterprise resource planning systems (ERP systems). In contrast to most other market reports this study gathered data from companies independently from ERP vendors and with a strong sample size. The sample size allows analyses regarding company size, region and sector. Additionally, special attention is given to implementation consultancies. The results show that the market shares differ from other European or global analyses. The information generated and market research carried out helps both, solution providers and companies in their strategic decision making process regarding target groups and ERP systems evaluations.

Keywords: ERP system · Market study · Implementation consultancy · Microsoft · SAP · Oracle · System evaluation

1 Introduction

The common answer to the question "Which is the most frequently used or implemented ERP system?" is "SAP". The stated question lacks a lot of specification from a researcher′s point of view. A diligent researcher would at least specify the geographical scope of the question: "Which is the most common ERP system globally or e.g. in a certain region or e.g. in a specific branch?" Additionally, who is actually interested in an answer to those questions? The information on the biggest ERP solution provider in a specific geographic location or business sector may be interesting to the system vendors themselves in order to satisfy their own and their stakeholders demand for data on market shares, potentials and expected future revenues. For enterprises considering an ERP implementation that information is also relevant however, the more details are available the more profound is the influence for a later decision making process. In this paper we will discuss why information on the market shares can be of relevance to

© Springer International Publishing Switzerland 2016
M. Felderer et al. (Eds.): ERP Future 2015 - Research, LNBIP 245, pp. 95–110, 2016.
DOI: 10.1007/978-3-319-32799-0_8

companies that plan to choose and implement a new ERP system and which level of detail of that information is required to create value in the evaluation process.

A huge amount of aspects have to be considered when selecting a "new" ERP system. The most important ones of course are the functionalities and modules of the solution itself and if it can actually cover the processes of the company to a necessary degree. Additionally experts recommend to consider cost and budget, service and support, technical criteria, scalability, performance, compatibility, portability, usability, market position, implementation methodology and references [1–4].

One aspect that is rarely explicitly stated is the question if a system is very common for companies of a certain industry, or of a certain size. However, this is one aspect that nearly always plays a major role as companies will gather information on which systems are used by the competitors. If this will affect the decision in favour of the most common system used by competitors ("if they use it, it must be good for our industry") or in the opposite direction ("if we want to be better we cannot use the same system") is not part of this paper.

Reliable information on market shares however is hard to find. Coming back to the opening question "What is the most frequently used or implemented ERP system for a certain industry in a certain country" the answer will very much depend on who you ask. If you enter the search term "most common ERP {country} {industry}" into www.google.com you will find differing results for nearly any combination of search terms. Usually the most successful players in a certain market, where market can be determined geographically, by industry or by size of the companies implementing the system, will all find a loop hole to justify the claim "XY is the most common choice for {small, medium, large} companies in the {finance, construction, …} industry" [5]. But can you really trust and rely on these statements? We do not intent to imply lying on purpose to anyone. However, all ERP providers do have their own and eligible interest in promoting their strength and maybe keep quiet about possible weaknesses or relativization. This implies that one should look for independent market studies, as they will provide more objective data [6, 7].

2   Purpose of this Study

The majority of market studies [8–10] in the field of ERP systems takes the system vendors or their reference customers as an entry point to deduct information. Its either revenues, amount of clients or amount of end-users which are most frequently used to determine the market share of each vendor. Each of those approaches has its advantage over other approaches for a certain purpose. However they all rely on data provided by system vendors who possibly have an interest in exaggeration or interpreting in their own favour. This again leads to results that might be influenced by certain interests of system vendors as they are providing the data for the studies.

This is the reason why we gathered data from the companies who have a system implemented. We believe that there is a lower risk for collecting wrong or biased information, as there is no purpose for companies to give false statements about the system they use. However we are aware that it is unlikely to be able to gather all data of the population, even not for a small investigated market. By gathering data from random companies in Austria we aim to provide a reliable overview on the Austrian ERP market and answer following research questions:

1. Which ERP systems are most frequently used in companies
    a. of a certain sector?
    b. of a certain size (amount of employees)?
    c. in a certain state?
2. Which implementation consultancies are most frequently active for companies
    a. of a certain sector?
    b. of a certain size (amount of employees)?
    c. in a certain state?
    d. implementing a specific ERP system?

3 Data Collection

To fulfil our approach in collecting data from random companies in Austria we took a random sample of 4,370 of a total of 502,159 companies listed at the "WKO Firmen A-Z" [11]. Companies with less than 2 employees were excluded from the interviews. A total of 3,582 companies participated in the survey. 788 companies were contacted but were not willing to answer the questions of the survey. Taking a confidence level of 5.00 % and confidence interval of 99.00 % for a representative market study under consideration a minimum of 663 participating companies would be needed. Due to the high number of ERP solutions on the market the survey was conducted with a significant higher number of participants to raise the representativity of the study. The data collection was conducted by telephone interviews following a structured questionnaire. The focus was clearly on a high quantity of participants but a low amount of queried items.

The classification and sectors as mentioned in Table 1 were deducted referring to ÖNACE 2008 [12] which itself is based on the European "Nomenclature européenne des activités économiques"(NACE) but extended to cover all Austrian specifications. ÖNACE has 615 classes in 88 sections which were reduced by the authors to the remaining 59 categories. The data collection took place from March to August 2014.

Table 1. Items of the survey

Item	Type	Options
Location of the company	closed	9 Austrian states
Amount of employees	open	
Sector	closed	service, trade, industry, public sector
Sector in detail	closed	59 categories
ERP system in use	open	
ERP system vendor	open	
Implementation consultancy	open	

4   Sample Descriptions

3,582 companies of the 4,370 contacted ones were willing to answer the questions on the phone. As Fig. 1 illustrates, the sample represents the geographical distribution of companies by Austrian states quite well. The geographical distribution of companies in Austria was derived from [11].

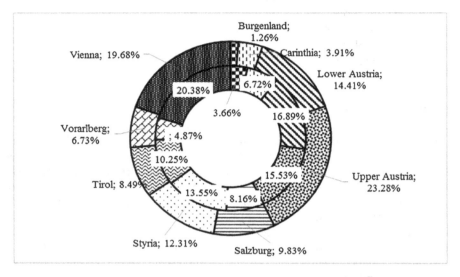

Fig. 1. Geographic distribution of companies: actual [11] (inner) and sample (outer; n = 3,582)

The same cannot be claimed concerning the size of companies (employees). A significant difference in the distribution of the amount of employees of participating companies compared to the actual one can be observed. Especially the category of 2-9 employees is underrepresented in our sample. Small companies might be generally less represented in the WKO data base. All other categories are overrepresented (Fig. 2).

As Fig. 3 illustrates about half of the participating companies are active in the industrial sector, followed by companies of the sectors "trade" and "services". Only less than 2 percent are active in the public sector.

During the interviews 140 different ERP systems were mentioned, of which the 15 most frequent ones are listed in Table 2. Unless the fact that MS Excel is not an ERP system by definition, it is listed since a high amount of interviewees replied MS Excel. The 15 most common systems in use cover a total of 65.64 % of interviewed companies.

From the statistics it is evident that not a single one or a few ERP systems dominate the Austrian market. The ERP market in Austria is divided among many providers. This applies particularly to 125 providers which share a third of the market.

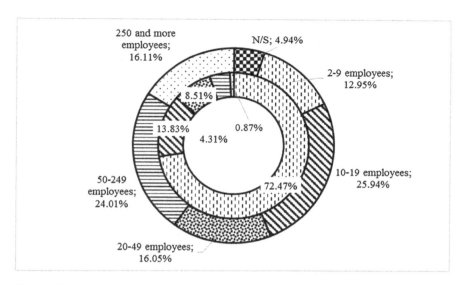

Fig. 2. Size of companies (employees): actual [11] (inner) and sample (outer; n = 2,582)

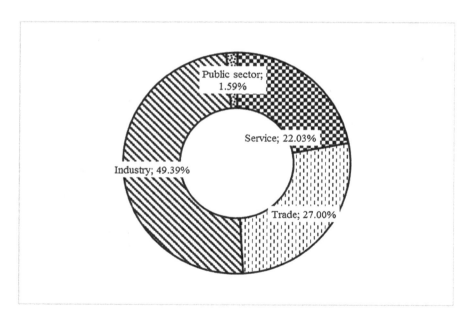

Fig. 3. Participants by sector (n = 3,582)

Table 3 indicates most frequent system vendors. The total coverage is even higher compared to the observation in Table 1 with 71.37 %. Would MS Excel and the related companies be excluded from the analysis, SAP Österreich GmbH would rank as first with 17.16 % followed by Microsoft Österreich GmbH with 11.03 % (Table 4).

Table 2. ERP systems in use: 140 in total; 15 most frequent ones listed

Rank	ERP system	Freq.	Percent	Cum.
1	MS Excel	627	17.50 %	17.50 %
2	SAP ERP	459	12.81 %	30.31 %
3	MS Dynamics NAV	213	5.95 %	36.26 %
4	NTCS	200	5.58 %	41.84 %
5	proAlpha	114	3.18 %	45.02 %
6	MS Dynamics AX	113	3.15 %	48.17 %
7	ORLANDO	112	3.13 %	51.30 %
8	rs2	80	2.23 %	53.53 %
9	Comtech Software	75	2.09 %	55.62 %
10	Win1A	70	1.95 %	57.57 %
11	TradeControl	69	1.93 %	59.50 %
12	abas ERP	57	1.59 %	61.09 %
13	Best*Line	57	1.59 %	62.68 %
14	BüroWare	53	1.48 %	64.16 %
15	Infor M3	53	1.48 %	65.64 %

Table 3. System vendors: 115 in total; 15 most frequent including Excel

Rank	System vendor	Freq.	Percent	Cum.
1	Microsoft Österreich GmbH	953	26.61 %	26.61 %
2	SAP Österreich GmbH	507	14.15 %	40.76 %
3	BMD SYSTEMHAUS GMBH	200	5.58 %	46.34 %
4	Infor Global Solutions GmbH	119	3.32 %	49.66 %
5	proALPHA Software Austria GesmbH	114	3.18 %	52.84 %
6	CPS Radlherr GmbH	112	3.13 %	55.97 %
7	Ramsauer & Stürmer Software GmbH	80	2.23 %	58.20 %
8	Comtech EDV-Organisations Gesellschaft	75	2.09 %	60.29 %
9	Schweighofer Manager-Software GmbH	71	1.98 %	62.27 %
10	PCS It-Trading GmbH	69	1.93 %	64.20 %
11	ABAS Software AG	57	1.59 %	65.79 %
12	Bertel Software	57	1.59 %	67.38 %
13	SoftENGINE GmbH	53	1.48 %	68.86 %
14	Asseco Germany AG	49	1.37 %	70.23 %
15	Mesonic Datenverarbeitung GmbH	41	1.14 %	71.37 %

The analysis of implementation consultancies shows a much more heterogeneous image. The 15 most common implementation consultancies among the 116 in total only cover 26.18 % of the observed market.

The providers SAP Austria GmbH and Microsoft Austria GmbH occur with exceptions not as implementation consultancies in the market. The question regarding the implementation consultancies could not be answered by some of the interviewees.

Table 4. ERP implementation consultancies: 15 most frequent

Rank	Implementation consultancies	Freq.	Percent	Cum.
1	SCC EDV Beratung GmbH	177	4.94 %	4.94 %
2	proALPHA Software Austria GesmbH	114	3.18 %	8.12 %
3	Ramsauer & Stürmer Software GmbH	80	2.23 %	10.35 %
4	Comtech EDV-Organisations GmbH	75	2.09 %	12.44 %
5	CNT Consulting GmbH	65	1.81 %	14.25 %
6	Nittmann & Pekoll GmbH	57	1.59 %	15.84 %
7	MBS - Modern Business Systems	54	1.51 %	17.35 %
8	Asseco Austria GmbH	49	1.37 %	18.72 %
9	Navax Consulting GmbH	48	1.34 %	20.06 %
10	Enigma IT-Systeme GmbH	38	1.06 %	21.12 %
11	ETRON Software GmbH	38	1.06 %	22.18 %
12	EASY SOFTWARE GmbH	37	1.03 %	23.21 %
13	PRO SOFT EDV GmbH	36	1.01 %	24.22 %
14	globesystems Business Software GmbH	35	0.98 %	25.20 %
15	POLLEX.-LC Software GmbH	35	0.98 %	26.18 %

Therefore, many potential implementation consultancies do not appear in the analysis. We therefore assume that the real numbers might be higher than the results of this study.

5 Analysis

The analysis is separated into two parts. The first set of research questions is concerned with the frequency of ERP systems applied in companies of a certain sector, a certain size or state. The second set of research questions is concerned with the implementation consultancies and their focus on sector, state and company size. Generally MS Excel was excluded from the following analyses.

5.1 Analysis on ERP Systems

Figure 4 demonstrates the distribution of the 10 most frequent observed systems in total in relation to the four distinguished sectors.

We observed that 7 out of the 10 most common systems have the majority of their customers in the industrial sector, which is of little surprise considering the composition of the sample. NTCS and Win1A seem to have their focus on the service sector, TradeControl as the name reveals on the trade sector.

Concerning NTCS, which is provided by BMD Systemhaus GmbH and has its origin in the field of accounting we can affirm two results of Fig. 4. NTCS is on the one hand in use by many tax advisers which explains the high share in the service sector. On the other hand many industrial companies which do not have an integrated ERP system implemented NTCS is used as an account system which speaks for the high share in the industry sector.

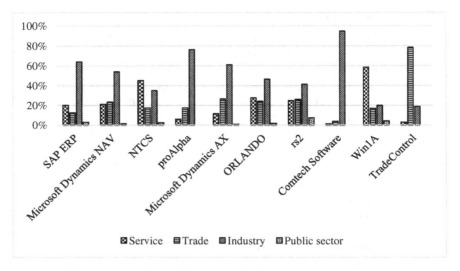

Fig. 4. Distribution of the 10 most frequent ERP systems by sector

To answer the question which ERP systems are most frequently used in companies of a certain sector we created Table 5 which lists the 10 most common systems for each sector. Systems that are among the top10 in every sector are highlighted in bold font.

In the next step we investigated the amount the popularity of ERP systems in relation to the size of interviewed companies. First we categorized companies in following classes:

- 2-9 employees: category 1
- 10-19 employees: category 2
- 20-49 employees: category 3

Table 5. Overview: most common ERP systems by sector

Service		Trade		Industry		Public Sector	
SAP ERP	93	**SAP ERP**	58	**SAP ERP**	294	**SAP ERP**	14
NTCS	90	TradeControl	54	**MS Dyn. NAV**	115	rs2	6
MS Dyn. NAV	45	**MS Dyn. NAV**	50	proAlpha	87	**NTCS**	5
Win1A	41	**NTCS**	35	Comtech Software	71	econdat	4
ORLANDO	31	Etron Software	33	**NTCS**	70	**MS Dyn. NAV**	3
Best*Line	25	MS Dyn. AX	30	MS Dyn. AX	69	WinLine	3
rs2	20	ORLANDO	27	ORLANDO	52	Win1A	3
easy2000	20	BüroWare	25	abas ERP	47	Etron Software	3
IGEL	15	retailONE	25	Infor M3	38	ORLANDO	2
StaffSupply	15	POLLEX-LC	25	APplus	38	easy2000	2

- 50-249 employees: category 4
- 250 and more employees: category 5

To find out if the majority of ERP systems are tailored to a certain company size we analysed the amount of categories that are served by a specific ERP system. Figure 5 shows that only 25 systems are used in all 5 categories concerning the amount of employees. 36 were found to be only present in 1 category.

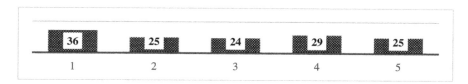

Fig. 5. Amount of categories (by company size) the ERP systems are used in

Table 6 shows which systems are the most common ones for a certain company size. We can observe a significant heterogeneity in this overview.

Table 6. Overview: most common ERP systems by company size

Smallest		Small		Medium		Large		Very large	
Win1A	37	ORLANDO	32	**MS Dyn. NAV**	45	SAP ERP	125	SAP ERP	261
ORLANDO	32	Comtech Software	30	**NTCS**	43	**MS Dyn. NAV**	83	**MS Dyn. NAV**	39
Best*Line	30	**NTCS**	21	ORLANDO	34	proAlpha	66	MS Dyn. AX	35
NTCS	30	**MS Dyn. NAV**	21	SAP ERP	31	**NTCS**	55	**NTCS**	33
Comtech Software	24	Best*Line	16	TradeControl	28	MS Dyn. AX	48	proAlpha	16
easy2000	22	BüroWare	15	proAlpha	25	abas ERP	31	Infor M3	15
retailONE	21	SAP ERP	12	rs2	19	rs2	28	rs2	13
BüroWare	20	Helium V ERP	10	Comtech Software	16	TradeControl	26	APplus	12
MS Dyn. NAV	16	globemanager plus®	10	Etron Software	15	Infor M3	26	Infor ERP LN	11
SAP Business ByDesign	11	profashion	9	MS Dyn. AX	13	APplus	23	abas ERP	10

Figure 6 illustrates the distribution of the 10 most frequently observed systems per state. On the first glance the high share of upper Austrian companies utilizing one of the most common systems can be observed. Comtech Software is very popular in Salzburg with significantly fewer customers in lower Austria, upper Austria and Vienna and no customers at all in the remaining states. All other top 10 systems do have customers in all states.

The 10 most commonly used systems are used primarily in the provinces of Vienna, Lower Austria and Upper Austria, where most companies are located.

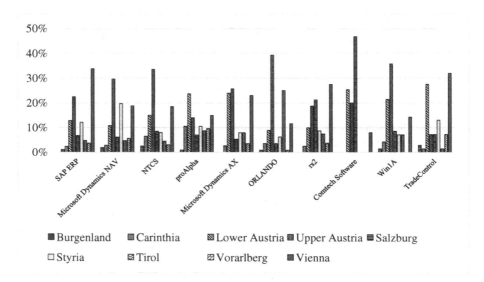

Fig. 6. Distribution of the 10 most frequent systems by state

5.2   Analysis on Implementation Consultancies

The second set of research questions is concerned with the implementation consultancies and their focus on sector, state and company size. Figure 7 illustrates the 10 most frequently observed implementation consultancies and the distribution of their clients concerning the sectors. The distribution of the clients of most of the listed implementation consultancies show a similar pattern compared to the composition of the entire sample – most in the industrial sector and about a quarter each in the trade and service sector, with only a few in the public sector. Exceptions are "Comtech EDV-Organisations GmbH" with a very strong focus on the industrial sector, similar to "Nittmann & Pekol GmbH" and "proALPHA Software Austria GesmbH". "ETRON Softwareentwicklung GmbH" on the other side has the vast majority of its customers in the trading sector.

By distinguishing between the most frequent implementation consultancies for each sector we can observe "SCC EDV Beratung GmbH" as the most successful one in all sectors except the trading sector which is led by "ETRON Software GmbH" (Table 7).

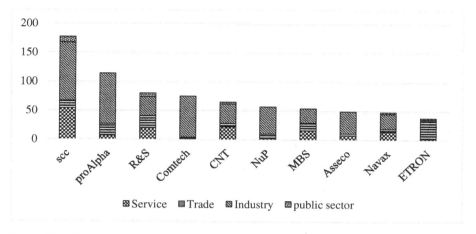

Fig. 7. Top 10 observed implementation consultancies in general stacked by sector (For full company name see appendix)

Table 7. Overview: most common implementation consultancies by sector

Service		Trade		Industry		Public sector	
scc	54	ETRON	33	**scc**	100	**scc**	10
CNT	22	PRO SOFT	30	proALPHA	87	**R&S**	6
EASY SW	20	Enigma	25	Comtech	71	Hainzl	4
R&S	20	POLLEX	25	NuP	47	CNT	3
MBS	16	**R&S**	21	Asseco	38	Navax	3
IGEL	15	proALPHA	20	CNT	34	ETRON	3
Prenner	15	**scc**	13	**R&S**	33	EASY SW	2
Navax	14	MBS	13	Navax	26	Datenpol	2
Future Factory	11	Globesystems	12	MBS	25	DSA	1
more Software	11	Scala	10	FWI	25	Helium V	1

Analyzing the activity of the most frequent stated implementation consultancies in relation to the amount of employees of their clients we can observe that 6 out of 10 find the majority of their customers in category 4 with 50 to 249 employees. "SCC EDV Beratung GmbH" and "CNT Consulting GmbH" have their focus on very large companies, whereas "Comtech EDV-Organisations GmbH" and "ETRON Software GmbH" are specialized on smaller companies as Fig. 8 illustrates.

Table 8 lists the most frequent implementation consultancies for each of the 5 company size categories. In comparison to the previous tables there is not a single player that is listed among the top 10 of each category. Among the 4 most frequently observed in total, "Ramsauer & Stürmer" is the only implementation consultancy that does not make it to the top of one category.

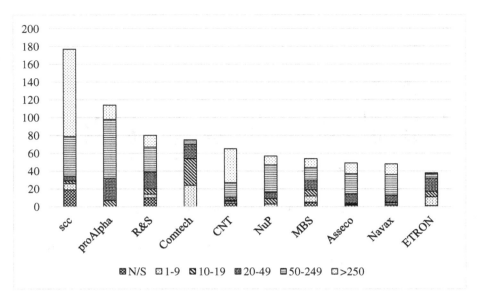

Fig. 8. Top 10 observed implementation consultancies in general stacked by size of clients (For full company name see appendix)

Table 8. Overview: most common implementation consultancies by company size

Smallest		Small		Medium		Large		Very large	
Comtech	24	Comtech	30	proALPHA	25	proAlpha	66	scc	98
Easy SW	22	Helium V	10	R&S	19	scc	45	CNT	38
Enigma	21	Globesystems	10	Comtech	16	NuP	31	proALPHA	16
PRO SOFT	11	PRO SOFT	9	ETRON	15	R&S	28	Fulcrum	16
Sumak	10	POLLEX	9	MBS	11	Asseco	23	R&S	13
ETRON	10	MBS	7	Globesystems	10	Navax	23	Asseco	12
Helium V	10	proALPHA	7	Asseco	10	terna	17	Navax	12
Globesystems	9	ETRON	6	PRO SOFT	9	CNT	16	FWI	12
More Software	9	More Software	6	Navax	8	Infor	16	NuP	10
Ninus	8	R&S	6	NuP	7	Data	15	MBS	10

The high level of specialisation of implementation consultancies to one specific ERP system is shown in Table 9. Among the 10 most frequently stated implementation consultancies only 2 were observed to work with a second ERP system and this only to a very low extent.

Table 9. Implementation consultancies and most frequent systems offered

Rank	Implementation consultancies	System	%
1	scc	SAP ERP	97.74 %
2	proALPHA	proAlpha	100.00 %
3	R&S	rs2	100.00 %
4	Comtech	Comtech Software	100.00 %
5	CNT	SAP ERP	96.92 %
6	NuP	Abas ERP	100.00 %
7	MBS	Microsoft Dynamics NAV	100.00 %
8	Asseco	APplus	100.00 %
9	Navax	Microsoft Dynamics NAV	100.00 %
10	ETRON	Etron Software	100.00 %

6 Results Compared to Other Studies

Similar studies for Austria do not exist. There are customer satisfaction surveys which are periodically conducted – mainly by system vendors – but they do not aim a comparison regarding market shares, neither in total nor on sectors or regions. Bender [13] released an ERP study in 2008 for Germany. It shows a market share of 51 % for SAP as the market leader. Microsoft Dynamics is ranked second with 6 %, Infor with 5 %, Sage with 4 % and Oracle with 3 %.

In 2013 Gartner [8] released the study "World Wide ERP Software Market Share, 2013" in which SAP is the market leader with 24 % compared to 17.16 % in the presented study, not taking MS Excel under consideration. Referring to Gartner Microsoft (without MS Excel) has a global market share of 5 % compared to 11.03 % in Austria. Oracle is in second place with 12 % on a global scale compared to a 0.47 % market share in Austria. Oracle has quite a different significance, especially in the USA, therefore studies are very difficult to compare on a global level because local ERP solution providers and vendors do not occur in global studies due to their limited market share on a global level. Another global ERP study shows similar results. In 2015 Panorama Consulting Solutions [14] conducted an analysis of ERP vendors which are shortlisted for tenders. In this study SAP is the market leader with 27 % followed by Oracle with 19 % and Microsoft with 13 % of the market. A problem identified within the reviewed studies is that by the indications it is not clearly marked which specific ERP systems is meant by the ERP product names Infor, Oracle, Microsoft, SAP and Sage. Since those vendors have several EPR solutions in their portfolios it would be valuable information.

The studies and the presented data show that SAP is undoubtable the market leader in ERP systems, globally as well as on a national level. Also Microsoft with its solutions Dynamics NAV and Dynamics AX has a strong position in all relevant studies. Still it has to be mentioned that the results also show that many globally unknown ERP vendors appear in the studies, but always with much lower market shares than the global players.

7 Conclusions

The goal of the presented study was to collect data to identify the most frequently used ERP systems and the most active implementation consultancies in Austria. The obtained data seems only be biased by the source of the addresses used since the sample does not represent the distribution regarding the amount of employees of the participating companies compared to the actual one. If this measure has a significant influence cannot be clarified within the study and needs further investigations. E.g. a second sample or a random reduction of the overrepresented categories of the existing sample to reach a similar distribution could be of valuable help to clarify this topic. The actual data is not sufficient to get representative results doing so. Therefore the authors are planning to collect further data until this representativeness is guaranteed.

With a closer look at the obtained data, it is obvious that the market leader for ERP systems is not Microsoft but SAP since MS Excel cannot be classified as an ERP system by definition. Still one has to take under consideration that the participants of the study use MS Excel functionalities as a substitute for an integrated ERP solution. Except for companies with less than 50 employees the spreadsheet hardly plays a relevant role. The study shows that with an increasing company size the usage and market share of SAP increases steadily. The distinct differences of the results with respect to the geographic regions can be explained to a large part by the size of the companies participating. However, there are some idiosyncrasies that are not attributable to the company size and therefore these are specific regional results. For example Comptech is overrepresented in west Austria.

Finally, it must be noted that in this study it was not possible to investigate the question of causality between size and industry. It is only observed that in this regard trends were identified. Additional data has to be collected and has to be analyzed in near future to give valid answers if trends are significant and if the bias mentioned above has an effect on the results presented in this study. Still the results of the study show quite a clear picture of the Austrian market for ERP systems respectively implementation consultancies and seem to be the first independent study conducted with a sample size of this level without involving ERP vendors themselves.

Appendix

Abbreviation	Full Name
Asseco	Asseco Austria GmbH
CNT	CNT Consulting GmbH
Comtech	Comtech EDV-Organisations GmbH
Datenpol	Datenpol GmbH
DSA	Data Systems Austria AG & Co KG
Easy SW	EASY SOFTWARE GmbH
Enigma	Enigma IT-Systeme GmbH

(*Continued*)

(*Continued*)

Abbreviation	Full Name
ETRON	ETRON Softwareentwicklungs- und Vertriebs GmbH
Fulcrum	Fulcrum Consulting GmbH
Future Factory	Future Factory Business SW GmbH
FWI	FWI Information Technology GmbH
Globesystems	globesystems Business Software GmbH
Hainzl	Ing. Johannes Hainzl GmbH
Helium V	Helium V IT-Solutions GmbH
IGEL	IGEL Software&Unternehmensberatung
Infor	Infor Global Solutions GmbH
MBS	MBS - Modern Business Systems Informationssysteme GmbH
More Software	more Software GmbH
Navax	Navax Consulting GmbH
ninus	Ninus Consulting GmbH
NuP	Nittmann & Pekoll GmbH
Pollex	POLLEX.-LC Software GmbH
Prenner	Ing. Gerhard Prenner
PRO SOFT	PRO SOFT EDV-Entwicklungs- und VertriebsgmbH
proAlpha	proALPHA Software Austria GesmbH
R&S	Ramsauer & Stürmer Software GmbH
Scala	Scala Software VertriebsgmbH
scc	SCC EDV Beratung GmbH
Sumak	Daniel Sumak
terna	terna GmbH

References

1. Asperion, P.M.: Funktionstrennung in ERP-Systemen, Konzepte, Methoden und Fallstudien, Wiesbaden (2013)
2. Haddara, M.: ERP Selection: The SMART Way. Procedia Technol. **16**, 394–403 (2014). CENTERIS 2014 - Conference on ENTERprise Information Systems / ProjMAN 2014
3. Schütte, R., Vering, O.: Erfolgreiche Geschäftsprozesse durch modern Warenwirtschafts systeme, Produktübersicht marktführender Systeme und Auswahlprozess, 3rd edn. Auflage, Heidelberg (2011)
4. Verville, J., Halingten, A.: A six-stage model of the buying process for ERP software. Ind. Mark. Manage. **32**, 585–594 (2003)
5. Ahmad, M., Pinedo-Cuenca, R.: Critical success factors for ERP implementation in SMEs. Robot. Comput.-Integr. Manuf. **29**, 104–111 (2013)
6. Perera, H., Costa, W.: Analytic hierarchy process for selection of ERP software for manufacturing companies. Vis. J. Bus. Perspect. **12**(4), 1–11 (2008)
7. Wu, L., Liou, F.: A quantitative model for ERP investment decision: considering revenue and costs under uncertainty. Int. J. Prod. Res. **49**(22), 6713–6728 (2011)

8. Pang, C., Dharmasthira, Y., Eschinger, C., Brant, K.F., Motoyoshi, K.: Market Share Analysis: ERP Software Worldwide 2013. Gartner (2013)

9. The 2015 ERP Report: A panorama consulting solutions research report. http://panorama-consulting.com/resource-center/2015-erp-report/. Accessed January 12 2016

10. Bender, S., Dobbert, D., Krühne, S., Röver, C.: Marktübersicht über ERP-Systeme und deren Anbieter. http://de.slideshare.net/ChrRoe/marktbersicht-erp-systeme. Accessed December 24 2015

11. WKO. https://firmen.wko.at/. Accessed June 12 2015

12. WKO. https://www.wko.at/Content.Node/Interessenvertretung/ZahlenDatenFakten/Oenace_2008_2014.html. Accessed June 12 2015

13. Bender, S., Dobbert, D., Krühne, S., Röver, C.: Marktübersicht über ERP-Systeme und deren Anbieter. http://de.slideshare.net/ChrRoe/marktbersicht-erp-systeme. Accessed June 12 2015

14. The 2015 ERP REPORT: A panorama consulting solutions research report. http://panorama-consulting.com/resource-center/2015-erp-report/. Accessed December 24 2015

Semantic Technologies for Managing Complex Product Information in Enterprise Systems

Bastian Eine[✉], Matthias Jurisch, and Werner Quint

RheinMain University of Applied Sciences, Unter Den Eichen 5, 65195 Wiesbaden, Germany
{Bastian.Eine,Matthias.Jurisch,Werner.Quint}@hs-rm.de

Abstract. Today, business transactions, including business processes and data management, are almost entirely electronic in nature. With regards to product information, enterprises are faced with the challenge of how to handle more and more information about products. Also, products information is getting more complex as enterprises tend to produce and offer more customizable products. Information systems of enterprises need functions based on specific technologies to be able to reduce and interpret the complexity of product information. This paper pursues the question, how the state of the art in information systems can be improved by the use of semantic technologies. For this purpose, three use cases of product information systems to be improved are described and approaches based on semantic technologies are proposed. The selected use cases are data integration, data quality and workflow integration.

Keywords: Product information management · Semantic technologies · Enterprise systems

1 Introduction

The establishment of electronic business processes brought a number of improvements for companies, e.g., automatic handling of purchasing and selling products. Therefore, data and information about products are almost exclusively managed in companies' information systems [1]. That being said, not all information systems have the ability to fully encompass the product information management (PIM) needs of a company. For example, Enterprise Resource Planning (ERP) systems are set up to represent all business processes of a company in order to increase the overall cost-effectiveness [2]. Often, ERP systems do not include product marketing descriptions, product pictures or complementary technical product data. Additionally, there are a number of other types of information systems, with which product information can be managed, e.g. Product Data Management Systems [3], Customer Relationship Management Systems [4], and Content Management Systems. [5]. Finally, PIM systems provide centralized and media neutral data storage, data management and data output of product information in companies [6]. PIM systems offer a number of functions, which enable companies to manage and use product information consistently in many areas inside and outside of the company. For instance, PIM systems can assist companies and employees with product

© Springer International Publishing Switzerland 2016
M. Felderer et al. (Eds.): ERP Future 2015 - Research, LNBIP 245, pp. 111–118, 2016.
DOI: 10.1007/978-3-319-32799-0_9

classification, translation management, media asset management and data output to different media (e.g., print catalogue, online shop, technical data sheets) [7].

However, companies have to handle more and more complex information about products as product complexity and customers demand for customizable products increases [8]. Also, many companies face the challenge of integrating product information that is scattered to many different information systems into one enterprise-wide, centralized PIM system. Today, many companies are not able to implement a PIM system into their information technology structure as processes for data integration are still too cost and time consuming for them. This can lead to redundancy of data and high inconsistency of product information in a company. Hence, high expenses for maintaining, searching for and presenting product information can arise [9]. Also, the number of customer requests and wrong orders and deliveries may increase. Therefore, it is necessary to implement syntactical, as well as semantical restrictions or defaults to avoid redundant statements or wrong interpretations.

Another challenge is to capture and represent complex product information, e.g., relations between products or product features. When composing a configurable product it has to be taken into account that selecting a certain product feature may exclude other product features. This information is essential for employees, who are responsible for maintaining product information but also for customers, who want to configure a product or satisfy their information need. Accordingly, it is necessary to capture, manage and present the information in a clear and easy to understand manner. Lastly, it has not yet been analyzed whether existing solutions take different user perspectives into account and if they do, how satisfying are they to the user.

We propose that the necessary data integration processes and the PIM systems can be improved by employing methods from the field of semantic technologies. This paper will analyze three use cases of product data integration and PIM system context that can be improved. Section 2 sketches the approach for using semantic technologies and summarizes the related work regarding PIM and semantic technologies. A detailed view on the use cases is presented in Sect. 3, while Sect. 3.1 covers data integration, Sect. 3.2 describes data quality measures and Sect. 3.3 gives an overview of workflow integration. A critical discussion of the approach is given in Sect. 4. The conclusion is presented in Sect. 5.

2   Approach and Related Work

The use of semantic technologies, when creating and representing complex information and relations between concepts, can help to interpret information by identifying the corresponding context. Semantic technologies can make it easier to understand the meaning and purpose of complex concepts as well as share knowledge for humans and machines [10]. For PIM, semantic technologies can be based on simple approaches like glossaries (lists of words and their definitions), taxonomies (hierarchies for terms) and thesauri (relations of similarity and synonyms) to avoid syntactical and semantic problems when creating and interpreting product information. Approaches with more semantic richness are topic maps [11] and ontologies [12].

Ontologies are usually defined as an "explicit specification of a conceptualization" [13]. This means that an ontology allows the definition of concepts and relationships between these concepts and that the specification representation provides a formal semantic of the specification. Usually, some kind of mathematical logic is used to provide the formal semantics of the specification, which allows the inference of new knowledge from the ontologies. Building on the ideas of ontologies, Berners-Lee et al. proposed the semantic web [14]. This idea is a technical approach applying ontology-based technologies to the web.

The semantic web has been adopted in various scientific domains. In bioinformatics, several ontology-based systems like the gene ontology [15] have helped researchers from different countries to communicate with each other and interlink their research data. A semantic web-based approach for integrating e-commerce systems has been proposed by Hepp [16] and since been adopted by search engines like Google and Yahoo.

Besides describing product information, these semantic technologies can be utilized also to capture and represent their relations and connections to other products, product components, product features and further information. With ontologies, it is also possible to represent rules, which are associated with the mentioned product relations. The solution of the problems described in this paper will enable the application of ontology-based approaches in the field of PIM that are new to this field.

One solution of the problems described in Sect. 1 would be the development of a new method based on semantic technologies. In this method, product information is modeled and represented using an ontology. Through the ontology, it will be possible to apply several methods from the field of semantic technologies that have not yet been adopted in PIM context before. The applied methods from semantic technologies are data integration through ontology alignment, data quality measurement, and workflow integration.

Previous research in these areas has shown that semantic technologies are applicable to the field of PIM. In 2005, the work by Hepp enabled the representation of eClass catalogues as an ontology by proposing a special ontology vocabulary named eClassOWL [17]. This work focused on representing the information from an eClass catalogue in an ontology. An overview of the possible improvements of PIM by semantic web technologies was given in 2007 by Brunner [18]. Brunner also presented a PIM system built on semantic technologies, while he concluded, that the semantic web technologies of that time did not allow the implementation of an efficient and scalable PIM system. Thus, proprietary extensions had to be applied. In 2008, Hepp presented the ontology GoodRelations as a semantic web-based representation for products and services [16]. Since then it has been adopted as a widespread method to annotate existing websites with product data that can be parsed by search engines like Google and Yahoo.

The Aletheia architecture is a work that focuses on the integration of structured and also unstructured data sources based on semantic technologies [19]. This approach is based on a service hub that allows data exchange and data transformation and separates between a certain and uncertain knowledge repository. Another integration-focused approach is presented in [20]. This work consists of a transformation from the standard catalogue format BMEcat to the already mentioned GoodRelations ontology.

A holistic approach for Master Data Management (MDM) is presented in [21]. The focus of this approach is the usage of the same data structures in different phases of the product life cycle. A research approach and preliminary results in the form of a reference architecture for a semantic MDM system are presented.

However, the technique of ontology alignment has not yet been applied to PIM systems and its applicability in this area has not yet been proven. It is expected that the application of ontology matching to complex product information structures will lead to a higher degree of automation of data integration. Also, this will contribute to the research about data integration approaches.

3 Application of Semantic Technologies to Product Information Management

3.1 Data Integration

Ontologies can be used to integrate data from heterogeneous data sources. Usually, this is done by creating a so-called ontology alignment (a highly simplified example is given in Fig. 1).

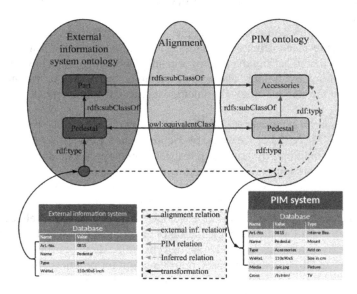

Fig. 1. Ontology alignment

This alignment contains the relationship between two data sources. Typical relationships between entities in the different data sources are equivalence (*owl:equivalent-Class*), subsumption (*rdfs:subClassOf*) and disjunction (*owl:disjointWith*). For example, this alignment can be used to generate a transformation between the data sources or to produce a mapping ontology that contains the relationship between them. Using this mapping ontology allows to infer the type for instances of the entities from all aligned data sources, like it is depicted for one record in the external information system in Fig. 1.

Alignments can be created manually, but it is also possible to generate them (semi-) automatically by a process called ontology matching. Ontology matching is a research topic that deals with integrating data from different sources by automatically (or semi-automatically) deducing the relationship between them [22]. Usually, ontology matching systems take two ontologies as input and provide the user with suggestions of correspondences between the data sources, which the user can accept or reject.

A technical challenge is the applicability of automated ontology matching to PIM. The current state of the art in ontology matching does not support the construction of complex alignments between ontologies to a satisfying degree [23]. Therefore, it has to be evaluated, whether PIM requires this type of alignments or simple alignments are expressive enough for PIM scenarios.

3.2 Data Quality

Another approach that is new to PIM is the integration of data quality measures. This will allow better assessment of the results of data integration than in previous PIM approaches. Also, this will support the evaluation of data integration results.

In information system research the Information System Success Model by DeLone and McLean is the most cited model that incorporates the concept of information quality [24]. The Information System Success Model helps to identify and understand information system success by six dimensions and their relationships: information quality, system quality, service quality, use of system and intention to use, user satisfaction, and net benefits of system. Information quality is regarded as a dimension to measure the semantic success of an information system [24]. From the consumer perspective Wang and Strong describe the concept of information quality as the "data that fit for the use by data consumers" (p. 6) [25]. According to DeLone and McLean information quality should be personalized, complete, relevant, easy to understand, and secure [25]. A theory to understand and also to predict technology acceptance is the Technology Acceptance Model by Davis et al. [27]. The Technology Acceptance Model implies that the perceived usefulness and the perceived ease of use of a system directly impact the attitude toward usage which then impacts the behavioral intent. While the Information System Success Model focuses on the net benefits associated with information system use, the Technology Acceptance Model focuses on expectations of net benefits from future information system use [28]. Hence, the Technology Acceptance Model and its application in PIM context can be taken into account for this research to measure the influence of product information quality on the perceived usefulness of the integration of product data and the PIM system itself.

For ontologies, several approaches that support data quality measurement exist in use cases like sensor networks [29], data integration [30] and representation of data quality constraints in general [31].

3.3   Workflow Support

Modeling product-related workflows through ontologies will also be incorporated into our method. Other approaches that model workflows in general are already existing. Standards for modeling workflows have also been transformed to ontologies as well. Garijo [32] presents an ontology for representing Open Provenance Model (OPM) workflows and Rospocher [33] describes an ontology for the Business Process Model and Notation (BPMN). This will allow a unified representation of product information and workflows related to it.

4   Discussion

A potential problem that could arise from the application of our method is caused by the complexity of the reasoning process in ontologies. This might lead to performance issues. These issues can be addressed by carefully selecting an ontology language that trades expressivity for reduced reasoning complexity.

Another potential shortcoming is the required initial training for developers who want to adopt this method. Also, the migration to an ontology-based implementation might induce high costs for the users. A cost-benefit-analysis of the conversion to our method is planned as a part of our future research to further investigate this question.

The method also offers several benefits. When the method is applied, the integration of new data sources into an existing system can be facilitated faster, easier and the results of the integration are easier to assess, too. The application of semantic-web-based methods might also improve the usability of software systems. Integration of semantics into the model itself also allows a decoupling of metamodels and implementation. Since the semantics of the metamodels of the data are part of the model, it can still be reused in other applications. When reusing the data, the meaning can be retained in the new application caused by the included specified semantics. This might also improve the maintainability of applications, because the semantics of the model are not encoded in the software but the model itself. Hence, the model semantics do not need to be fully understood by the developers that maintain the software.

5   Conclusion

In this paper, we have presented three use cases for product data integration and PIM systems that could be improved by the employment of semantic technologies. The use cases are data integration from internal and external sources, data quality measurement and improving workflow support. Existing research covering the specific problems of these use cases has been presented for each of the use cases.

For data integration, a method called ontology matching has been proposed. This method allows the semi-automatic generation of alignments. Alignments are used to formalize the coherence between ontologies. For data quality, approaches for evaluating product information quality and data integration quality were referenced. Also, two examples of approaches for workflow support have been mentioned.

These ideas have not yet been evaluated for their practical applicability. For future research, each of the approaches will have to be evaluated through a prototype implementation and a user study, to measure their effectiveness and usability. This research is part of the proposed research project PIMonto, which is currently in the process of being evaluated by the Eurostars funding agency. If the project proposal is granted, the research will start in the beginning of 2016.

References

1. O'Brien, J.A., Marakas, G.: Management Information Systems. McGraw-Hil/Irwin, New York (2011)
2. Sumner, M.: Enterprise Resource Planning. Prentince Hall, Indiana (2005)
3. Philpotts, M.: An introduction to the concepts, benefits and terminology of product data management. Indus. Manage. Data Syst. **96**(4), 11–17 (1996)
4. Ngai, E.W.T.: Customer relationship management research (1992-2002): an academic literature review and classification. Mark. Intell. Plan. **23**(6), 582–605 (2005)
5. Boiko, B.: Content Management Bible. Wiley, New York (2001)
6. Gartner Magic Quadrant for Product Information Management 2007. ftp://public.dhe. ibm.com/software/emea/de/db2/Gartner_MDM_Magic_Quadrant_PIM.pdf
7. Lucas-Nülle, T.: Product Information Management in Deutschland - Marktstudie 2005. Pro-Literatur-Verl. Mayer-Scholz, Mammendorf (2005)
8. Sheldon, P., Goetz, M.: The Forrester Wave: Product Information Management, Q2 2014. https://www.informatica.com/resources.asset.84dbaa93b4463fbae96a596b2068676d.pdf
9. Gartner Magic Quadrant for Product Information Management 2005. http://whitepapers. zdnet.com/abstract.aspx?docid=258733
10. Pellegrini, T., Blumauer, A.: Semantic web und semantische technologien. In: Pellegrini, T., Blumauer, A. (eds.) Semantic Web - Wege zur vernetzten Wissensgesellschaft, pp. 9–25. Springer, Berlin (2006)
11. Pepper, S.: The TAO of Topic Map - Finding the Way in the Age of Infoglut. http://www.onto-pia.net/topicmaps/materials/tao.html
12. Gruber, T.: Toward principles for the design of ontologies used for knowledge sharing. Int. J. Hum.-Comput. Stud. **43**(5–6), 907–928 (1995)
13. Gruber, T.: Ontology. http://tomgruber.org/writing/ontology-definition-2007.htm
14. Berners-Lee, T., Hendler, J., Lassila, O.: The semantic web. Sci. Am. **284**(5), 28–37 (2001)
15. Ashburner, M., Ball, C.A., Blake, J.A., Botstein, D., Butler, H., Cherry, J.M., Sherlock, G.: Gene ontology: tool for the unification of biology. Nat. Genet. **25**(1), 25–29 (2000)
16. Hepp, M.: GoodRelations: an ontology for describing products and services offers on the web. In: Gangemi, A., Euzenat, J. (eds.) EKAW 2008. LNCS (LNAI), vol. 5268, pp. 329–346. Springer, Heidelberg (2008)
17. Hepp, M.: eClassOWL: a fully-fledged products and services ontology in OWL. In: 4th International Semantic Web Conference (ISWC2005) (2005)
18. Brunner, J.S., Ma, L., Wang, C., Zhang, L., Wolfson, D. C., Pan, Y., Srinivas, K.: Explorations in the use of semantic web technologies for product information management. In 16th International Conference on World Wide Web, pp. 747–756. ACM (2007)
19. Wauer, M., Schuster, D., Meinecke, J.: Aletheia: an architecture for semantic federation of product information from structured and unstructured sources. In: 12th International Conference on Information Integration and Web-based Application and Services, pp. 325–332. ACM (2010)

20. Stolz, A., Rodriguez-Castro, B., Hepp, M.: Using BMEcat catalogs as a lever for product master data on the semantic web. In: Cimiano, P., Corcho, O., Presutti, V., Hollink, L., Rudolph, S. (eds.) ESWC 2013. LNCS, vol. 7882, pp. 623–638. Springer, Heidelberg (2013)
21. Fitzpatrick, D., Coallier, F., Ratté, S.: A holistic approach for the architecture and design of an ontology-based data integration capability in product master data management. In: Rivest, L., Bouras, A., Louhichi, B. (eds.) PLM 2012. IFIP AICT, vol. 388, pp. 559–568. Springer, Heidelberg (2012)
22. Euzenat, J., Shvaiko, P.: Ontology Matching. Springer, Heidelberg (2013)
23. Otero-Cerdeira, L., Rodriguez-Martinez, F.J., Gomez-Rodriguez, A.: Ontology matching: a literature review. Expert Syst. Appl. **42**(2), 949–971 (2015)
24. Delone, W.H., McLean, E.R.: The DeLone and McLean model of information systems success: a ten-year update. J. Manage. Inf. Syst. **19**(4), 9–30 (2003)
25. Wang, R.Y., Strong, D.M.: Beyond accuracy: what data quality means to data consumers. J. Manage. Inf. Syst. **12**(4), 5–34 (1996)
26. Delone, W.H., Mclean, E.R.: Measuring e-commerce success: applying the DeLone & McLean information systems success model. Int. J. Electr. Commer. **9**(1), 31–47 (2004)
27. Davis, F., Bagozzi, P., Warshaw, P.: User acceptance of computer technology - a comparison of two theoretical models. Manage. Sci. **35**(8), 982–1003 (1989)
28. Wang, Y.: Assessing e-commerce systems success: a respecification and validation of the DeLone and McLean model of IS success. Inf. Syst. J. **18**(5), 529–557 (2008)
29. Esswein, S., Goasguen, S., Post, C., Hallstrom, J., White, D., Eidson, G.: Towards ontology-based data quality inference in large-scale sensor networks. In 12th International Symposium on Cluster, Cloud and Grid Computing (Ccgrid 2012), pp. 898–903. IEEE Computer Society (2012)
30. Martin, N.: A methodology and architecture embedding quality assessment in data integration. J. Data Inf. Qual. **4**(4), 17 (2004)
31. Fürber, C., Hepp, M.: Towards a vocabulary for data quality management in semantic web architectures. In: 1st International Workshop on Linked Web Data Management (LWDM 2011), pp. 1–8 (2011)
32. Garijo, D., Rey, M.: A new approach for publishing workflows: abstractions, standards, and linked data. In 6th workshop on Workflows in Support of Large-Scale Science, pp. 47–56 (2011)
33. Rospocher, M., Ghidini, C., Serafini, L.: An ontology for the business process modelling notation. In: 8th International Conference (FOIS 2014), p. 133. IOS Press (2014)

IT-Trends

Research Challenges of Industry 4.0 for Quality Management

Harald Foidl[1(✉)] and Michael Felderer[2]

[1] exceet electronics GesmbH, 6341 Ebbs, Austria
harald.foidl@exceet.at
[2] Institute for Computer Science, University of Innsbruck,
6020 Innsbruck, Austria
michael.felderer@uibk.ac.at

Abstract. By promising huge benefits for industries and new opportunities for a multitude of applications, Industry 4.0 is currently one of the major and most discussed topics in academia and practice. Beside this trend, today's manufacturing companies have to produce products of highest quality in order to retain competitive and satisfy the steadily increasing customer requirements. Thus, an essential prerequisite and key to sustainable economical success for any company is to focus on quality management. Through its concepts (Smart Factory, Cyber-Physical System, Internet of Things and Services), Industry 4.0 provides promising opportunities for quality management. Therefore, this paper presents research challenges of Industry 4.0 for quality management motivated by a practical insight of an Austrian electronic manufacturing services company. The presented research challenges are structured by the three key aspects of Industry 4.0 (vertical, horizontal and end-to-end engineering integration) and grounded on the DIN ISO 9000 quality management systems approach.

Keywords: Industry 4.0 · Smart factory · Internet of Services · Cyber-Physical System · Internet of Things · Quality management · Quality · Integration · Research challenges · Quality management systems approach

1 Introduction

First mentioned as a key strategic initiative of the German federal government's High-Tech Strategy 2020 action plan in 2011 [1], Industry 4.0 became a high relevant and frequent discussed topic for companies, universities and research centers [2, 3]. The buzzword Industry 4.0 [2] describes the fourth, currently taking place [3], industrial revolution which promises huge economical potential as well as provides promising ecological and social opportunities [4]. Moreover, Industry 4.0 and its current concepts (i.e. Smart Factory, Cyber-Physical System (CPS), Internet of Things (IoT) and Internet of Services (IoS)) [5] also cause a paradigm shift in work organization [6], business models [1] and production technology [7]. The factory of the future is characterized by smart, interconnected, integrated and real-time oriented processes and services [1, 8]. These characteristics enable on the one hand a vertical integration of the smart factory's IT systems in order to ensure flexible, dynamically reconfigurable

© Springer International Publishing Switzerland 2016
M. Felderer et al. (Eds.): ERP Future 2015 - Research, LNBIP 245, pp. 121–137, 2016.
DOI: 10.1007/978-3-319-32799-0_10

and self-organized manufacturing systems and structures [1, 9]. Essential part of this vertical integration is the linkage of sensor and actuator signals through various levels right up to the level of the Enterprise Resource Planning (ERP) system [1, 9]. On the other hand, manufacturing and information systems in such smart and networked factories are not only networked within the factory but also connected to value networks and supply chains [1]. These digital networks across the company's boundaries are mainly based on a tight interconnection of Enterprise Resource Planning systems and Manufacturing Execution systems (MES) [8]. As a result, systems in the factory of the future have to deal with an enormous amount of data and must share a large volume of information with each other [8, 10].

According to Mittelstädt et al. [11], the above mentioned concepts of Industry 4.0 offer, behalf an increase of productivity and quantity, also a promising potential for the domain of quality management by increasing the quality of products, processes and services. Due today's manufacturing industries must operate in an intense competitive and highly sophisticated global environment, the pressure on them to offer higher product quality at lowest costs and within the shortest possible time to satisfy customers and retain their position in the market, continuously increases [12]. Accordingly, the key to success and an indispensable requirement to gain global market share for any manufacturing company is to focus on quality management [12]. As a result of the Industry 4.0 driven shift of responsibility and awareness from the manufacturing process to the product itself [7], the product becomes a smart and interacting key element in the information infrastructure of manufacturing companies [13]. By capturing and processing product and quality information [13], the smart product enables automatic monitoring and context awareness which results in a performance increase of IT systems across different levels up to the Enterprise Resource Planning system [14]. Production as well as quality management could use these new gathered information and data for better decision-making and evaluation of the organization's processes [13]. Especially, since modern quality management not only means to avoid the delivery of defect products but rather seeks to ensure high performance with maximum efficiency of all processes of an organization [12], Industry 4.0 and its concepts provide promising opportunities and chances for the domain of quality management. In addition, a survey of 235 German industrial companies showed that companies expect far-reaching qualitative benefits of Industry 4.0 (i.e. more than 80 % expect a high or moderate effect on improved quality through Industry 4.0) [15]. Hence, this paper has the objective to identify research challenges of Industry 4.0 for quality management.

The remainder of this paper is structured as follows. Section 2 presents background information on Industry 4.0 and its main concepts. Afterwards, Sect. 3 gives a brief overview of the field of quality management. Section 4 then illustrates the potential and opportunities of Industry 4.0 from the context of an Austrian electronic manufacturing services company. Motivated by this practical insight, Sect. 5 presents research challenges of Industry 4.0 for quality management. The presented research challenges are grounded on the DIN ISO 9000 quality management systems approach and are structured by the three key aspects of Industry 4.0 (vertical, horizontal and end-to-end engineering integration). Finally, Sect. 6 summarizes and concludes the paper.

2 Industry 4.0

As a result of the introduction of water- and steam-powered mechanical manufacturing facilities, the first industrial revolution began at the end of the 18th century [1]. Electrically-powered mass production and the division of labor led to the second industrial revolution at the end of the 19th century [1]. From the early 1970 s on, the usage of information technology and advanced electronics for the further automation of manufacturing resulted in the third industrial revolution [1]. Now, the fourth industrial revolution is the first revolution which is proclaimed before it takes place [16]. Accordingly, many companies and research institutes (i.e. Working Group Industry 4.0 [17], Plattform Industrie 4.0 [18], Industrie 4.0 Collaboration Lab [19]) are actively trying to contribute to the fourth industrial revolution in order to shape the future [3]. Due to this enormous contribution which resulted in various articles, papers and discussions, the term and the idea behind Industry 4.0 became unclear and are often misunderstood [16]. Although the Working Group Industry 4.0 describe a comprehensive vision of Industry 4.0, mention eight priority areas in which further research and development is needed for a successfully implementation of Industry 4.0 as well as describe the basic technologies behind the vision and present selected Industry 4.0 implementation scenarios, they do not provide a clear definition of the term Industry 4.0 [1, 3]. Hermann et al. [3] address this gap and provide the following definition of Industry 4.0 based on a comprehensive literature review:

> "*Industrie 4.0 is a collective term for technologies and concepts of value chain organization. Within the modular structured Smart Factories of Industrie 4.0, CPS monitor physical processes, create a virtual copy of the physical world and make decentralized decisions. Over the IoT, CPS communicate and cooperate with each other and humans in real time. Via the IoS, both internal and cross-organizational services are offered and utilized by participants of the value chain.*"

This definition compromises four basic concepts of Industry 4.0 (Smart Factory, CPS, IoT and IoS) [3] which are explained in the following in order to illustrate the concepts and ideas behind the fourth industrial revolution.

Drath [16] describes the vision of Industry 4.0 on an abstract level as "the embedding of internet technologies in the industry". The IoT as a kind of internet technology refers in a general way to "the networked interconnection of everyday objects [...] via embedded systems" [20]. Therefore, people, devices, things and objects form a highly distributed network incorporating the entire manufacturing process [1, 20]. In the context of Industry 4.0, CPSs can communicate and cooperate through the IoT and offer relevant data and information in the network [21]. By offering and selling services [22], the IoS even goes one step further. Services can for example combine the available data of all networked objects and provide new opportunities which where not (economically) feasible before [16]. In addition, services can be linked to other services and be further offered [16], beside the intra-factory participants, also to participants along the entire value chain which leads to a variety of new business models [1].

The Working Group Industrie 4.0 grounded their vision of Industry 4.0 on **Cyber-Physical Systems** [1]. Such systems comprise production facilities, storage systems and smart machines which trigger actions, exchange information complete autonomously and are able to control each other independently [1]. Resulting, companies can connect and incorporate their production facilities, warehousing systems and machinery as CPSs in the context of global networks [1]. In detail, CPSs can be seen as a new generation of systems which merge the physical and the cyber world [16] by integrating "computational and physical capabilities that can interact with humans through many new modalities" [23]. Resulting, CPSs compromise several "collaborating computational entities which are in intensive connection with the surrounding physical world and its on-going processes" [24]. Further, CPSs build the basis to connect the different kinds of internet technologies (IoT, IoS and also the Internet of "People") [25]. According to Majstorović et al. [24] the usage and deployment of CPSs in manufacturing companies enables the concept of "Smart Factory". Lucke et al. [26] define a **Smart Factory** as "a Factory that context-aware assists people and machines in execution of their tasks". This can be realized by CPSs which are able to interact and communicate with its environment by using data and information from the physical as well as the virtual world, and as a result consider this context information for the accomplishment of their tasks [3, 26].

The factory of the future is fully equipped with actors, sensors and CPSs [5, 26] and provides an environment where "human beings, machines and resources communicate with each other as naturally as in a social network" [1]. Moreover, the factory of the future will "partly break with the traditional automation pyramid" [27]. Through the usage of CPSs in the smart factory, the strictly separated automation hierarchy (which is shown on the left side of Fig. 1) will be replaced by decentralized, self-organized and networked services (right side of Fig. 1) [27, 28]. Data, functions and services are available for each entity in the CPS and each entity can start interacting with each service [29]. Therefore, the functional scope of the classical automation pyramid is actually not replaced but rather preserved and even expanded [30] in order to seamlessly connect the different levels [8]. As a result, decisions are not further made at the peak of the automation pyramid but at the lowest possible level under consideration of defined rules [2]. This means that the collection of process data is not further restricted to the lowest field level but rather possible for all entities through the initiation of services [28]. Furthermore, reactions can be implemented with the shortest distance to the initiator which results in an increase of flexibility and productivity [31].

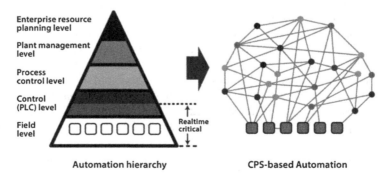

Fig. 1. Decomposition of the automation pyramid [26, 27]

Although the successive replacement of the automation pyramid by decentralized, self-organized and networked services [28], the ERP system as former peak of the automation pyramid, still have its place in the smart factory [8]. Optimizing business decisions, ensuring the transparency of global processes as well as the orchestration of manufacturing via a network of global production sites and through inter-company networks will still be the core tasks of ERP systems [8]. In order to fulfill these tasks and to deal with the huge amount of different data formats, protocols and interfaces which result from the high number of variable and decentralized production processes, a high degree of standardization is necessary [8].

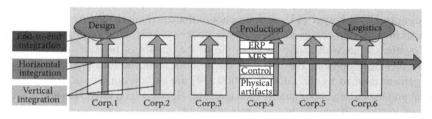

Fig. 2. Industry 4.0 integration aspects [9]

Concluding, Industry 4.0 will focus on the following three key aspects as presented by the Working Group Industry 4.0 [1] (Fig. 2 graphically sketches the three aspects):

- Vertical integration and networked manufacturing systems
  Vertical integration refers to the creation of flexible and reconfigurable manufacturing systems by the seamless integration of the hierarchical systems inside a company [1, 9].
- Horizontal integration through value networks
  The horizontal integration aims to create inter-corporation collaborations which result in an efficient ecosystem where material, information, energy and finance can flow fluently between several different companies [1, 9]. All data which describe the current state of the value chain will be available and can be used to control the value stream in an optimal way [16].
- End-to-end digital integration of engineering across the entire value chain
  The last kind of integration is based on the first two and aims to create a powerful software tool chain which enables the usage of a consistent product model at every stage of the value chain (i.e. engineering, design, planning, services and maintenance). This tool chain enables smart factories to foresee the effects of product design on production and hence makes it feasible to manufacture customer individual products [1, 9].

3   Quality Management

Nowadays, the quality of products, services and processes is essential to achieve sustainable economic success and to ensure competitiveness [32]. As an important area of research and practice, quality management has attracted the interest of many academics and managers [33].

Increasing customer expectations, global competition and the continuous increasing complexity of products are the reasons why quality management has become indispensable in today's companies and quality became an integral part of corporate objectives, strategies and policies [35]. Due to the fact that the term "quality" is used in different ways and means different things to different people [35, 36], several definitions and concepts for quality (i.e. Crosby [37], Garvin [38], DIN EN ISO 9000 [34]) exist. Resulting, also quality management, as a very subjective concept for which several approaches and philosophies (i.e. Total Quality Management (TQM) [39, 40], Zero Defects Concept [41], Quality Management principles defined by the DIN EN ISO 9000 [34]) exist, is hard to define [12, 42]. In this paper, quality management is seen, according to Hehenberger [43], as a functional management discipline which seeks to optimize business processes and workflows under consideration of physical and temporal restrictions as well as the preservation of the quality of products or services and their further development. Furthermore, the authors think the four concepts of quality management defined by the DIN ISO 9000 [34] are an appropriate mean to provide a general understanding about quality management. Hence, Fig. 3 illustrates and describes the four quality management concepts (quality planning, quality control, quality assurance and quality improvement) and their relation to effectiveness, efficiency and continual improvement.

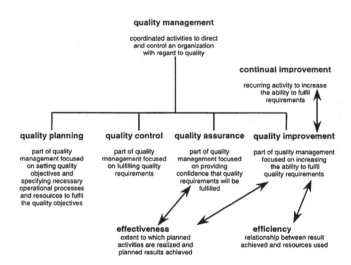

Fig. 3. Quality management concepts [34]

4 Industry 4.0 from a Practical Context

The following section outlines the chances, potentials and challenges of Industry 4.0 from the perspective of exceet electronics GesmbH. Exceet electronics GesmbH is an electronic manufacturing services company focusing on industrialized and automated development and manufacturing of high-quality and complex electronic modules, components and systems. The business area comprises the medical technology sector, semiconductor industry, automation sector, shipping industry as well as energy and environmental technology sector. Exceet electronics GesmbH[1] is part of the international technology group exceet Group SE and incorporated in the business sector "Electronic Components, Moduls and Systems". [44] In the context of exceet, Industry 4.0 provides several opportunities to improve and strengthen the current business. Grounded on informal interviews with three key stakeholders of the company (quality manager, production manager and process engineer), the remainder of this section outlines these opportunities. The opportunities, which are presented in the following, reflect the personal and subjective opinion of exceet and are structured by the three key aspects of Industry 4.0: vertical integration (Sect. 4.1), horizontal integration (Sect. 4.2) and end-to-end engineering integration (Sect. 4.3). Finally, Sect. 4.4 summarizes the main Industry 4.0 driven opportunities in the context of exceet.

4.1 Vertical Integration

As a full-service outsourcing company, exceet offers the complete value creation from the initial idea to the finished product. Based on the variety of different and customized products, exceet's manufacturing environment is characterized by several stand-alone solutions which perform distributed and complex production steps (i.e. assembly of printed circuit boards, equipment manufacture). By a *seamless integration and interconnection of all different production processes and steps*, exceet expects more transparency of its production processes coupled with less required effort. Through the *usage of sensors at each production stage*, exceet sees the chance to reach a new level of identifying quality related causes and issues which should reduce scrap and rework. As a result of connecting different systems, new daily production and business metrics can be available in real time and provide the necessary information to change and adjust processes or resources without delay. In addition, networked processes and machinery should enable a preventively acting in case undesirable events are approaching. Resulting, responsible persons should immediately be notified about occurring problems in the manufacturing workflow and causes of problems should be easily identifiable based on the new gathered data and information (i.e. which solder profile leads to quality issues). Through the *tight networking of all machines and products*, quality related information about failures and problems can be shared between the machines and the machines can immediately inform the operator. This would address the common problem of information sharing between people working in different shifts.

Exceet further sees the chance to optimize the sequences of its production processes by implementing CPSs which *virtually represent all physical products, machines and resources*. A lot of electronical components are moisture sensitive and therefore must be immediately welded after usage. An optimized production sequence where several smart products communicate and "book" their optimal way through the manufacturing process [16] (considering the most efficient utilization of resources (i.e. family setups)),

---

[1] In the remainder of the paper just named "exceet".

could bring immense benefits to the company. One further benefit of the tight vertical networking of all machines is the reduction of communication and interface problems between production machinery. Currently, machines are typically connected through different manufacturer-specific interfaces (i.e. SMEMA machine interface standard [45]) which strictly limit the transfer of data and information. By connecting machinery through the IoT and over the IP protocol, exceet sees on the one hand the chance to connect machines which are not communicating yet and on the other hand the possibility to break up the current restricted data exchange between machines.

Exceet already connected its ERP system with its manufacturing and process controlling system. Through this integration, the ERP system does not print delivery notes for products which failed during internal testing. This implemented process interlock acts as a *smart activity tracker* which monitors the different testing steps and only enables the ERP system to print the delivery note when all testing steps required for a product are executed in the right order and did not fail.

4.2   Horizontal Integration

A main improvement which exceet foresees in the horizontal integration of the value chain is to better integrate its customers and suppliers. Today, many customers have to call in order to get informed about the current state of their ordered product. By a *tight horizontal integration of all systems along the entire value chain* customers are able to track the progress of their ordered product. At any time, a customer can get the current status of the product in the manufacturing process and can see which tasks are already fulfilled and which are coming next. In case of problems, the customers can be immediately informed and provided with actual data in order to decide how to deal with the arising problem. Moreover, today's complex products are often changed during the manufacturing process. Especially in the context of manufacturing electronic modules, where a diversity of complex components are mounted and soldered, changes occur frequently. Based on a *close integration of the customer in the manufacturing process*, changes and change requests can be handled in a better way and the customer is able to trigger the changes at the desired stage in the production process. In addition, the customer immediately gets feedback about the effects of changes and can regulate, for example in case of problems, the lot size for the next production step. Moreover, customer's developers and engineers are highly interested in data of test results and how their developed products behave in the different stages of production (i.e. results of function tests, solder profiles). Through a close cooperation, enabled by a horizontal integration of manufacturing systems with the customer's system, developers and engineers can analyse the behavior of their products at each production stage and are able to react very quickly to undesired outcomes. Beside these opportunities, customers also can profit in the context of complaints and required quality assessments. Feedback on complaints can be handled much faster and in much more detail (i.e. providing exact used production parameters which led to the complaint) and the customer immediately can monitor the taken counter measures in the production process.

The horizontal integration is not only beneficial to the customer. Exceet also assumes a high potential to optimize the flow of goods when suppliers get real time information about the actual stocks of in-house components and future demand. Therefore, suppliers can better plan and organize the delivery and immediately share the information if components are not available any more. Due to the immense variety of different components on today's complex electronic modules and devices, many suppliers deliver the necessary amount of components for one product. A *networked integration of different suppliers* enable the chance to reduce missing parts and to avoid money tied up in stocks because production processes typically only start if all necessary components have arrived at the factory. Moreover, suppliers and manufacturers of components directly get data of how their components and parts perform in the manufacturing processes (i.e. defects and waste of a component relating to applied solder temperature profile). This enables suppliers to optimize their product portfolio and manufacturers to improve their components in accordance with real manufacturing data.

4.3 End-to-End Digital Integration of Engineering

By an end-to-end digital integration of engineering, exceet sees the opportunity to reduce the currently huge amount of data transformations along the life cycle of a product. The *digital incorporation of each stage* of a product's life cycle enables new synergies and opportunities to optimize engineering along the entire value chain of a product. Products can carry relevant information and data about themselves (i.e. assembly plan, circuit plan, production parameters) on their own (i.e. product memory [46]) and can provide this information at each stage of their life cycle. Further, exceet expects a reduction of time to market of new products if engineers and developers can use complete digital models and simulations of the manufacturing process and therefore are able to foresee the results and effects of their product designs.

4.4 Summary

Summarizing, exceet awaits huge potential provided by the different concepts of Industry 4.0. Through implementing concepts of Industry 4.0, exceet sees the chance to fundamentally improve the entire production planning, optimize the flow of goods, optimize the quality of processes and products, strengthen the customer and supplier relationships as well as the potential of offering new business models. Moreover, exceet expects a further automation of its processes and a high level of digitalization which should make the lives of people easier and reduce their workload. In addition, exceet anticipates a noteworthy decrease of the entire manufacturing lead time and simultaneously a reduction of buffer stock as well as the elimination of overproduction through implementing an Industry 4.0 driven decentralized and self-organized manufacturing structure. Apart from these chances, exceet thinks the main upcoming challenges are filtering and processing the huge amount of new information which is provided by Industry 4.0 in order to avoid information overload. A further challenge which exceet foresees is the determination of the defined rules in which the autonomous smart machines and systems can decide on their own. For example, a lot of processes in the medical industry have to fulfill stringent requirements and are validated based on defined conditions. Therefore, the range of freedom for each smart device must be carefully determined to ensure compliance to the regulations.

5 Research Challenges

In this section, the authors discuss potential research challenges for the quality management domain which arise through Industry 4.0. Whereas Industry 4.0 is in the following represented by its three key aspects, the quality management domain is represented by the eight steps of the quality management systems approach defined by the DIN ISO 9000 [34]. Concretely, the DIN ISO 9000 [34] lists eight steps to develop, implement, maintain and improve an existing quality management system. As a first step, the European Standard mentions the determination of needs and expectations of customers and other interested parties [34]. Second, an organization's quality policy and quality objectives should be established [34]. Third, processes and responsibilities, which are necessary to attain quality objectives, have to be determined [34]. In addition, appropriate resources should be determined and provided in order to ensure the attainment of the quality objectives [34]. Further, methods to measure the efficiency and effectiveness of each process must be established and applied [34]. Moreover, means should be determined in order to prevent nonconformities and eliminate their causes [34]. Lastly, a process of continual improvement for the quality management system should be established and applied [34]. The authors think the eight steps to implement and improve a quality management system are an appropriate mean to construct a linkage between Industry 4.0 and the quality management domain since they are neither too abstract nor too detailed to act as a basis for formulating research challenges (the corresponding step is stated after each challenge in parentheses).

Besides debating research challenges *of* Industry 4.0 for the quality management domain, another interesting point of view would be to debate the research challenges *for* Industry 4.0 in order to support the quality management domain. Both points of view can, in the opinion of the authors, not be strictly separated. In the remainder of this section, the authors focus on the first point of view and discuss research challenges for the quality management domain structured by the three Industry 4.0 key aspects: vertical integration (Sect. 5.1), horizontal integration (Sect. 5.2) and end-to-end engineering integration (Sect. 5.3). The following presented research challenges are motivated by the practical insight outlined in Sect. 4. In addition, the statements of the practical insight are further underpinned with current literature in order to provide a solid basis to formulate research challenges. Figure 4 illustrates on the right side the eight steps of the quality management systems approach and on the left side the three key aspects of Industry 4.0. The two-sided arrow in the middle of Fig. 4 represents the two points of view mentioned above.

5.1 Vertical Integration

Through the comprehensive and tight networking of all machines, resources and products inside the factory of the future as well as along the entire value chain, the

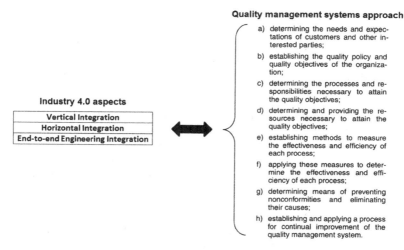

Fig. 4. Research Challenges of Industry 4.0 for Quality Management [based on 34]

fourth industrial revolution is characterized by a huge volume of aggregated data [47]. Due the new available data combines and aggregates data from different sources, which was not possible in the past [48], there are several possibilities for the quality management domain to use this new information. Processing and filtering these huge portion of data in order to provide useful and transparent information, which are understandable for humans, is according to Mayer and Pantförder [47] an upcoming challenge. For the quality management domain these new emerging potential of richer information enables, for example, the new generation of performance indicators for monitoring and tracking the manufacturing processes [49]. Furthermore, also the concept of virtual quality management (vQM) can benefit from the usage of this new information. The concept of vQM typically considers, in addition to the provided information from all machines and products, also environmental factors that can have a potential influence on the product [50]. By simulation and modelling, quality and process parameters can be obtained and further be optimized [50, 51]. Moreover, vQM also provides the opportunity to test and optimize virtual process chains already before the real processes are set up in the factory [51]. Hence, the availability of new data provided by all interacting machines and products provides huge potential for the vQM (i.e. precise prognoses, enhanced quality stamp of each product's way through the manufacturing process incorporating fabrication tolerances).

Moreover, the aspect of vertical integration enables the opportunity to transfer quality control and diagnostic data from the shop floor directly to each decision making level and vice versa [52] which in turn supports the ERP system in optimizing the entire manufacturing management [53]. In addition, concepts of Industry 4.0 provide the possibility of advanced diagnostics (i.e. backward reasoning [53]) and a higher degree of machine-condition awareness which enables a new area of predictive maintenance [52, 54]. Further, people can be better supported when they get additional information assistance for completing their working tasks [55] (i.e. avoidance of defect generation through augmented reality and virtual tools [52]). Moreover, through RFID the traceability of products throughout each manufacturing stage provides the possibility to correlate any error to its causing production step and therefore improves quality error management and fault diagnostics [52, 56]. This enables a fast and situation adapted reaction of decision makers. Based on these statements, following research challenges for the quality management domain arises:

1. *How can the huge volume of data and information, evolving through Industry 4.0, be used for establishing and applying methods to measure the efficiency and efficacy of each important process in an organization?* (*e, f*)
2. *How can the huge volume of data and information, evolving through Industry 4.0, be used for determining means of preventing nonconformities and eliminating their causes?* (*g*)

By applying advanced data mining techniques on these new data, new patterns, structures, interdependency and explanatory models [57] of the manufacturing process can be identified (i.e. bottlenecks through insufficient working instructions or operator know-how) which in turn can be used for a better determination of necessary resources (i.e. more skilled personnel, trainings). Hence, following research challenge arises:

3. *How can the huge volume of data and information, evolving through Industry 4.0, be used for enhancing the determination of resources necessary to attain the quality objectives?* (*d*)

In addition, Lee et al. [53] mention that smarter machines in the factory of the future are able to adjust production parameters and actively suggest operation arrangement in order to maximize product quality. Based on this decentralization and autonomy of the smart machines and products in the smart factory, following research challenge for the quality management domain arises:

4. *Which quality related measures must be taken, do define and regulate the limits of the rules, in which the machines and products can act and decide on their own, in order to be compliant with existing quality policies and objectives?* (*b*)

According to the DIN ISO 9000 [34], the analysis and evaluation of the existing situation is an important activity in the continual improvement process of a quality management system. With regard to the opportunities provided by Industry 4.0, following research challenge arises:

5. *How can the seamless virtual integration and collaboration of all machines, resources and products, in the context of CPSs, be used for enhancing the process of continual improvement?* (*h*)

5.2   Horizontal Integration

Based on the horizontal integration aspect of Industry 4.0, there arise several new business models for companies [28]. For example, customers can use services to trace and monitor their ordered products in real time in order to exactly know the current state of their order. This enables customers to place last-minute requests for changes which can immediately be incorporated during production [1]. Following, a close horizontal integration enables a product- and customer specific coordination of all activities along the entire value chain [1]. By talking about quality in these new evolving horizontal value networks, it is also important to incorporate suppliers [58]. Enabled by concepts of Industry 4.0, manufacturing machines easily can connect to cloud-based platforms where they can download relevant and required functions and data [1]. Moreover, smart machines can search online for appropriate experts who can perform maintenance with knowledge platforms and other enhanced engineering methods directly from a central telepresence portal [1]. Based on these statements, following research challenge for the quality management arises:

6. *How can the new evolving inter-corporation collaborations be used for better determining the needs and expectations of customers and suppliers? (a)*

According to Sila et al. [58] it is very difficult and challenging to manage quality along globalized value chains because typically every participant has specific capabilities and quality related goals. Therefore, following research challenge evolves:

7. *Which quality related measures must be taken to ensure that all participants along the new emerging tight horizontal value chain contribute to the organizational quality policy and objectives? (b)*

5.3 End-to-End Engineering Integration

According to Kagermann et al. [1] the concept of CPS enables a modelled and digital end-to-end methodology that "covers every aspect from customer requirements to product architecture and manufacturing of the finished product". This resulting end-to-end engineering tool chain makes it possible to manufacture customer individual products [1]. Moreover, also the already mentioned concept of vQM, which obtains process and quality parameters through simulation and modelling [50], can profit in several ways by an end-to-end integration of engineering. As a result, the model and simulation oriented integration of engineering inspires following research challenge:

8. *How should engineering processes and responsibilities be organized along an end-to-end digital integration of engineering in order to contribute to the quality policies and to attain the quality objectives? (c, b)*

6 Conclusion

Today's companies have to operate in a highly competitive environment where the quality of their processes, services and products mainly determines their economical success, market share and future [12]. Not surprisingly, the domain of quality management has become an integral and indispensable part of corporate management for every company [35]. By providing huge economical, ecological and social potential

[4], Industry 4.0 further provides promising opportunities for quality management. Since ERP systems can be seen as software applications for controlling and tracking transactions [59], they contain a lot of data which are essential for quality management to utilize the provided opportunities of Industry 4.0. Based on this and considering that ERP systems and quality management are complementary resources which are both necessary to improve the organizational performance and to gain competitive advantage [59, 60], one can argue that ERP systems will play an important role for quality management to address the upcoming research challenges of Industry 4.0. In this paper, the authors presented research challenges of Industry 4.0 for quality management. First, a compact overview of the main concepts (Smart Factory, CPSs, IoT and IoS) and aspects (vertical, horizontal and end-to-end engineering integration) of Industry 4.0, followed by a brief introduction of the quality management domain, was provided. Afterwards, the authors outlined Industry 4.0 and its potential from the context of an Austrian electronic manufacturing services company. Then this practical insight was used as motivation to formulate research challenges of Industry 4.0 for the quality management domain. Due the practical insight is limited based on a company from one specific industry, the authors tried to address this limitation by underpinning the statements of the practical insight with current literature in Sect. 5 to ensure a solid basis to formulate research challenges. The finally presented research challenges are further grounded on the DIN ISO 9000 [34] quality management systems approach and structured by the three key aspects of Industry 4.0 (vertical, horizontal and end-to-end engineering integration).

The contribution of this paper is twofold. On the one hand the authors want to provide a general understanding about the upcoming challenges and opportunities for the quality management domain through the advent of Industry 4.0. On the other hand the authors aim to provide a solid basis for further research in this area by formulating research challenges which can be used by academics to derive concrete research questions for future research.

References

1. Kagermann, H., Wahlster, W., Helbig, J.: Recommendations for implementing the strategic initiative INDUSTRIE 4.0 - Final report of the Industrie 4.0 Working Group (2013)
2. Dais, S.: Industrie 4.0 - Anstoß, Vision, Vorgehen. In: Bauernhansl, T., Ten Hompel, M., Vogel-Heuser, B. (eds.) Industrie 4.0 in Produktion, Automatisierung und Logistik, pp. 625–634. Springer Vieweg, Wiesbaden (2014)
3. Hermann, M., Pentek, T., Otto, B.: Design Principles for Industrie 4.0 Scenarios: A Literature Review. Working Paper No. 01/2015, Technische Universität Dortmund - Fakultät Maschinenbau, Audi Stiftungslehrstuhl Supply Net Order Management (2015)
4. Kagermann, H.: Chancen von Industrie 4.0 nutzen. In: Bauernhansl, T., Ten Hompel, M., Vogel-Heuser, B. (eds.) Industrie 4.0 in Produktion, Automatisierung und Logistik, pp. 603–614. Springer Vieweg, Wiesbaden (2014)
5. Lasi, H., Kemper, H.-G., Fettke, P., Feld, T., Hoffmann, M.: Industry 4.0. Bus. Inform. Syst. Eng. **04**, 239–242 (2014)

6. Hartmann, E.A.: Arbeitsgestaltung für Industrie 4.0: Alte Wahrheiten, neue Herausforderungen. In: Botthof, A., Hartmann, E.A. (eds.) Zukunft der Arbeit in Industrie 4.0, pp. 9–20. Springer Vieweg, Berlin (2015)
7. Valdez, A.C., Brauner, P., Schaar, A.K., Holzinger, A., Ziefle, M.: Reducing complexity with simplicity - usability methods for industry 4.0. In: 19th Triennial Congress of the International Ergonomics Association (2015)
8. Kleinemeier, M.: Von der Automatisierungspyramide zu Unternehmenssteuerungs-netzwerken. In: Bauernhansl, T., Ten Hompel, M., Vogel-Heuser, B. (eds.) Industrie 4.0 in Produktion, Automatisierung und Logistik, pp. 571–579. Springer Vieweg, Wiesbaden (2014)
9. Wang, S., Wan, J., Li, D., Zhang, C.: Implementing smart factory of industrie 4.0: an outlook. Int. J. Distrib. Sens. Netw. **2016**, Article ID 3159805, 10 p (2016). doi:10.1155/2016/3159805
10. Constantinescu, C.L., Francalanza, E., Matarazzo, D., Balkan, O.: Information support and interactive planning in the digital factory: approach and industry-driven evaluation. Procedia CIRP **25**, 269–275 (2014)
11. Mittelstädt, V., Brauner, P., Blum, M., Ziefle, M.: On the visual design of ERP systems – the role of information complexity, presentation and human factors. Procedia Manufact. **00**, 270–277 (2015)
12. Singh, M., Khan, I.A., Grover, S.: Tools and techniques for quality management in manufacturing industries. In: National Conference on Trends and Advances in Mechanical Engineering, pp. 853–859 (2012)
13. Putnik, D.G., Varela, R.L., Carvalho, C., Alves, C., Shah, V., Castro, H., Ávila, P.: Smart objects embedded production and quality management functions. Int. J. Qual. Res. **9**, 151–166 (2015)
14. Bajic, E.: A service-based methodology for RFID-smart objects interactions in supply chain. Int. J. Multimedia Ubiquit. Eng. **4**, 37–56 (2009)
15. Geissbauer, R., Schrauf, S., Koch, V., Kuge, S.: Industry 4.0 - Opportunities and Challenges of the Industrial Internet (2014)
16. Drath, R.: Industrie 4.0 - eine Einführung. open automation 3/14, 16–21 (2014)
17. Working Group Industry 4.0. https://www.bosch-si.com/solutions/manufacturing/industry-4-0/working-group.html
18. Plattform INDUSTRIE 4.0. http://www.plattform-i40.de/
19. Industrie 4.0 Collaboration Lab. https://www.imi.kit.edu/2449.php
20. Xia, F., Yang, L.T., Wang, L., Vinel, A.: Internet of things. Int. J. Commun Syst **25**, 1101–1102 (2012)
21. Lee, I., Lee, K.: The internet of things (IoT): applications, investments, and challenges for enterprises. Bus. Horiz. **58**, 431–440 (2015)
22. Cardoso, J., Voigt, K., Winkler, M.: Service engineering for the internet of services. In: Filipe, J., Cordeiro, J. (eds.) Enterprise Information Systems. LNBIP, vol. 19, pp. 15–27. Springer, Heidelberg (2009)
23. Baheti, R., Gill, H.: Cyber-physical systems. In: Samad, T., Annaswamy, A. (eds.) The Impact of Control Technology, pp. 161–166. IEEE Control Systems Society (2011)
24. Majstorović, V.D., Mačužić, J., Šibalija, T.V., Ercevic, M., Ercevic, B.: Cyber-Physical Manufacturing Systems – Towards New Industrialization. XVI International Scientific Conference on Industrial Systems (IS 2014), Novi Sad, Serbia (2014)
25. Bauernhansl, T.: Die Vierte Industrielle Revolution - Der Weg in ein wertschaffendes Produktionsparadigma. In: Bauernhansl, T., ten Hompel, M., Vogel-Heuser, B. (eds.) Industrie 4.0 in Produktion, Automatisierung und Logistik, pp. 5–35. Springer Vieweg, Wiesbaden (2014)

26. Lucke, D., Constantinescu, C., Westkämper, E.: Smart factory - a step towards the next generation of manufacturing. In: Mitsuishi, M., Ueda, K., Kimura, F. (eds.) Manufacturing Systems and Technologies for the New Frontier: The 41st CIRP Conference on Manufacturing Systems, pp. 115–118. Springer, New York (2008)
27. Monostori, L.: Cyber-physical production systems: roots, expectations and R&D challenges. Procedia CIRP **17**, 9–13 (2014)
28. Bettenhausen, K., Kowalewski, S.: Cyber-Physical Systems: Chancen und Nutzen aus Sicht der Automation. VDI/VDE-Gesellschaft Mess- und Automatisierungstechnik (2013)
29. Hoppe, S.: Standardisierte horizontale und vertikale Kommunikation: Status und Ausblick. In: Bauernhansl, T., ten Hompel, M., Vogel-Heuser, B. (eds.) Industrie 4.0 in Produktion, Automatisierung und Logistik, pp. 324–341. Springer Vieweg, Wiesbaden (2014)
30. Pötter, T., Folmer, J., Vogel-Heuser, B.: Enabling Industrie 4.0 - Chancen und Nutzen für die Prozessindustrie. In: Bauernhansl, T., ten Hompel, M., Vogel-Heuser, B. (eds.) Industrie 4.0 in Produktion, Automatisierung und Logistik, pp. 159–171. Springer Vieweg, Wiesbaden (2014)
31. Trenner, T., Neidig, J., Findeisen, R., Streif, S.: Einsatz cyber-physischer Systeme im Echtzeitkontext. In: Automation 2014, pp. 311–324. (2014)
32. Müller, E.: Qualitätsmanagement für Unternehmer und Führungskräfte. Springer, Berlin (2014)
33. Peris-Ortiz, M., Álvarez-García, J., Rueda-Armengot, C.: Achieving Competitive Advantage through Quality Management, p. 312. Springer, Cham (2015)
34. ISO: Quality management systems - Fundamentals and vocabulary (ISO 9000:2005) (2005)
35. Brüggemann, H., Bremer, P.: Grundlagen Qualitätsmanagement. Springer Vieweg, Wiesbaden (2012)
36. Lovelock, C., Wirtz, J.: Services Marketing: People, Technology, Strategy. Pearson, New Jersey (2007)
37. Crosby, P.B.: Quality is Free: The Art of Making Quality Certain. McGraw-Hill, New York (1979)
38. Garvin, D.A.: What Does 'Product Quality' Really Mean? MIT Sloan Manage. Rev. **26**, 25–48 (1984)
39. Feigenbaum, A.V.: Total quality control. Harvard Bus. Rev. **34**, 93–101 (1956)
40. Feigenbaum, A.V.: Total Quality Control. McGraw-Hill, New York (1991)
41. Crosby, P.B.: Z is for Zero-Defects. Industrial Quality Control, pp. 182–185 (1964)
42. Saraiva, M., Novas, J.C., Gomes, P.G.: How communication and control processes improve quality. In: Peris-Ortiz, M., Álvarez-García, J., Rueda-Armengot, C. (eds.) Achieving Competitive Advantage through Quality Management, pp. 219–231. Springer, Cham (2015)
43. Hehenberger, P.: Computerunterstützte Fertigung. Springer, Heidelberg (2011)
44. exceet electronics. http://www.exceet-electronics.com/
45. Surface Mount Equipment Manufacturers Association. http://www.dynamixtechnology.com/docs/smema1.2.pdf
46. Faltinski, S., Henneke, D., Jasperneite, J.: M2M communication using RF-ID and a digital product memory. In: 5. Jahreskolloquium "Kommunikation in der Automation" (KommA) (2014)
47. Mayer, F., Pantförder, D.: Unterstützung des Menschen in Cyber-Physical-Production-Systems. In: Bauernhansl, T., ten Hompel, M., Vogel-Heuser, B. (eds.) Industrie 4.0 in Produktion, Automatisierung und Logistik, pp. 481–491. Springer Vieweg, Wiesbaden (2014)
48. Forstner, L., Dümmler, M.: Integrierte Wertschöpfungsnetzwerke - Chancen und Potenziale durch Industrie 4.0. In: Elektrotechnik & Informationstechnik, vol. 131, pp. 199–201. Springer, Wien (2014)

49. Aehnelt, M., Bader, S.: Tracking assembly processes and providing assistance in smart factories. In: Proceedings of the 6th International Conference on Agents and Artificial Intelligence (ICAART), Angers, France (2014)
50. Bodi, S., Popescu, S., Drageanu, C., Popescu, D.: Virtual Quality Management elements in optimized new product development using genetic algorithms. In: Joint International Conference: Managing Intellectual Capital and Innovation for Sustainable and Inclusive Society - Management, Knowledge and Learning - Technology, Innovation and Industrial Management, Bari, Italy, pp. 633–642 (2015)
51. Bookjans, M., Weckenmann, A.: Virtual Quality Management - Validation of measurement systems by the use of simulation technologies. Phy. Procedia 5, 745–752 (2010)
52. Colledani, M., Tolio, T., Fischer, A., Iung, B., Lanza, G., Schmitt, R., Váncza, J.: Design and management of manufacturing systems for production quality. CIRP Annals - Manufacturing Technology 63, 773–796 (2014)
53. Lee, J., Kao, H.-A., Yang, S.: Service innovation and smart analytics for Industry 4.0 and big dataenvironment. Procedia CIRP 16, 3–8 (2014)
54. Schöning, H., Dorchain, M.: Data Mining und Analyse. In: Bauernhansl, T., ten Hompel, M., Vogel-Heuser, B. (eds.) Industrie 4.0 in Produktion, Automatisierung und Logistik, pp. 543–554. Springer Vieweg, Wiesbaden (2014)
55. Aehelt, M., Bader, S.: Tracking assembly processes and providing assistance in smart factories. In: Proceedings of the 6th International Conference on Agents and Artificial Intelligence (ICAART), Angers, France (2014)
56. Scholz-Reiter, B., Freitag, M.: Autonomous processes in assembly systems. CIRP Ann. Manufact. Technol. 56, 712–729 (2007)
57. Wieland, U., Pfitzner, M.: Interdisziplinäre Datenanalyse für Industrie 4.0. Controlling Manage. Rev. 58, 80–85 (2014)
58. Sila, I., Ebrahimpour, M., Birkolz, C.: Quality in supply chains: an empirical analysis. Supply Chain Manage. Int. J. 11, 491–502 (2006)
59. Laframboise, K., Reyes, F.: Gaining competitive advantage from integrating enterprise resource planning and total quality management. J. Supply Chain Manage. 41, 49–64 (2005)
60. Sánchez-Rodríguez, C., Martínez-Lorente, A.R.: Effect of IT and quality management on performance. Ind. Manage. Data Syst. 111, 830–848 (2011)

Security-Based Approach for Transformations of Mobile Accesses to ERP Systems

Kurt Porkert[⊠] and Gunther Marquardt

Fakultät Wirtschaft und Recht, Hochschule Pforzheim, Tiefenbronner Straße 65,
75175 Pforzheim, Germany
kurt.porkert@hs-pforzheim.de,
gunther.marquardt@t-online.de

Abstract. The characteristics and the levels of mobile accesses to ERP systems are changing differently in companies. Three proposed approaches assist with individual transformation of mobility concepts. A classification concept of basic access variants facilitates to identify the current mobility level and advantageous transformation paths. A process model describes how a two-stage feasibility check can be integrated in security analyses and decision-making for an iterative access transformation. A chart gathers the main criteria of the feasibility check for pre-defined security controls. They are used to estimate whether the mobility objectives can be reached with acceptable security risks by the transformation step.

Keywords: ERP system · Mobility · Transformation · Information security

1 Introduction

Mobile accesses to ERP systems and other application systems are indicated by a mobility of the devices, the users and the services [1]. They are coupled with attractive benefits as well with significant problems and risks for information security and privacy [2–4]. Companies therefore restrict these mobile accesses more or less powerfully. This paper classifies typical characteristics of mobile ERP system accesses. The classification criteria result from access scenarios that are described in publications or identified by author's own investigations.

The transformation of mobile access solutions into variants having a higher level of mobility presupposes decisions. Published proposals for decision aspects are especially the enterprise readiness [5], the stages of the transformation process [2, 5], the acceptance of the solution [6] or the perception of the benefits [7]. The paper presents an approach to include information security into transformation decisions for the ERP system access. The basis is a security analysis concept for individual transformation steps that considers the classified levels of mobility. It contains a two-stage feasibility check of transformation variants. The criteria of the checking should relate to the transformation objectives, information security, compliance, the necessary efforts, financing and other conditions.

© Springer International Publishing Switzerland 2016
M. Felderer et al. (Eds.): ERP Future 2015 - Research, LNBIP 245, pp. 138–146, 2016.
DOI: 10.1007/978-3-319-32799-0_11

2   Classification of Mobile Access Variants for ERP Systems

The mobility transformations of ERP system accesses are associated with the intention to enable special benefits of modified access scenarios, primarily increased flexibility. Such a scenario represents the realized or desired mobility levels for typical mobility aspects of the ERP system access (see Table 1).

Table 1. Aspects and levels of mobile ERP system accesses

Limitation of	Levels of mobile accesses		
Access locations	Intra-company	Local remote	Flexible remote
Device types	Portables	Mobiles	Wearables
Device sponsors	Company	Mixed sponsorship	Employee
Device liability	Company	Mixed liability	Employee
Device models	Take this device	Choose your device	Bring any device
Users	Selected employees	All employees	External users
Offline copies	Not permitted	Limited	Not limited
Application execution	Centralized	Mixed	Local
Private uses	Not permitted	Limited	Not limited
Business applications	Not permitted	Non-sensitive data	Sensitive data
ERP system components	Limited use	Full use	Enhanced use
Data access	Limited access	Full access	Enhanced access
User permissions levels	Read permission	Write permission	Admin. permission

Several mobility levels are described in numerous publications. Examples are:

- Access locations: "Internally Mobile", "Home Office", "Remote Mobile" [8]
- Device types: "Laptop", "Tablet/Smartphone" [1, 9], "Wearable Computing" [10]
- Device sponsors: "Corporate-Owned Device", "Bring Your Own Device", "Corporately Sponsored Private Device" [11],
- Device liability: "Corporate-Owned, Personally Enabled" [4], "Corporately Unmanaged Arbitrarily Device Model", "Corporately-Approved Device Model", "Corporately Managed and Approved Device Model" [12]
- Device models: "Take This Device/Choose Your Device/Bring Any Device" [13]
- Users: "Internal Users", "External Users" [2], "Occasional Users", "Professional Users", "Ubiquitous Users" [14, 15]
- Offline copies: "Centralized Data Modes", "Local Data Modes" [4], "Mobile Offline Mode" [16–18], "Thin-Clients", "Fat-Clients" [2]
- Application execution: "Virtual Desktop", "Session Virtualization", "Web App", "Application Virtualization", "Native Application", "Virtual Machine" [4]
- Private uses: "Bring Your Own App" [15, 19, 20], "Bring Your Own Service" [4]
- Business applications: "Mobile Access the Internet via the Organization's Network Infrastructure", "Mobile Access Non-sensitive Data", "Mobile Access Sensitive Data", "Mobile Access Highly Sensitive Data" [12]

- ERP system components: "Field Sales and Customer Service", "Mobile Production Control", "Mobile Warehouse Management", "Mobile Maintenance" [2, 17, 21]
- Data access: "Mini-ERP-Apps" [22], "Full ERP Access" [23]
- User permissions levels: "Mobile Reporting", "Mobile Data Capture" [17].

The ERP-access scenarios in enterprises are changing in stages. The access transformation paths proceed in certain step sequences which look similar in many companies [2, 12, 13, 15]. Often companies allow several mobility levels for one mobility aspect, for example, both "Take This Device" and "Choose Your Device". Currently, however, most companies strongly restrict the mobility levels of their ERP system accesses, which is evidenced by numerous surveys. This is caused by the disadvantages of the increasingly complex access scenarios. These disadvantages include primarily additional threats to information security. The security risks tend to be higher with rising flexibility of access scenarios. The resulting risks should be taken into account in decisions concerning the ERP access transformations. The objective is the greatest possible flexibility in a level of security risks tolerated by the company. Therefore decisions regarding the ERP mobility scenarios should be combined with information security analyses.

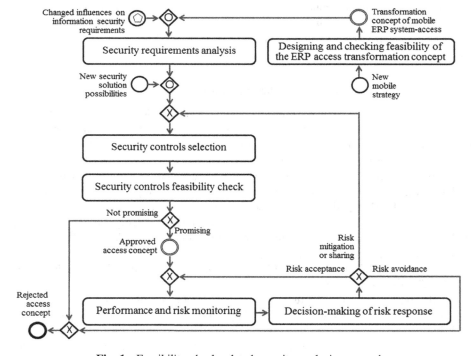

Fig. 1. Feasibility check related security analysis approach

3 Security Analysis for Mobile ERP Access Transformations

Different enterprise security approach patterns [24–26] describe steps of information security analyses. From the pattern of BSI [26] for the creation of a security concept, the authors derive a proposal (Fig. 1) to combine this analysis with a two-stage feasibility check for transformations of the mobile ERP system access.

Table 2. Exemplary security vulnerabilities and security controls for mobility aspects

Levels of mobile access for	Related supplementary security vulnerabilities (examples)	Related supplementary security controls (examples)
Access locations	Network exploits, data interception, lost, stolen or damaged device, stolen data	VPN, remote deletion, locking and locating of a lost device, policies for losses, thefts and forbidden access locations
Device types	Unauthorized use (photography, filming) of devices, limited device-specific security techniques	Device-specific policies and training, privacy film
Device sponsors	Pitfalls of licensing, tax law, employment law, liability, maintenance and support	Agreements with employees, providers of device software, apps, maintenance and support
Device models	Insufficient know-how of specific threats and security controls, operating system limitations	Whitelists of permissible device models
Device liability	Unsupported operating systems or anti-virus software, inept protection against threats	Policies for patch management, automated scans of devices, agent checking, quarantine network
Users	Uninformed, untrained or malicious users	User types classifying, rules of conduct, user behavior monitoring
Offline copies	Lost or stolen data	Thin clients, encrypted locally stored data, data synchronization policies
Application execution	Malicious local software, stolen or adulterated data	Thin clients, application allocation policies
Private uses	Malicious applications and services, violation of privacy	Data container, virtual machines, policies for private use, blacklists of harmful software and services
Business applicat. ERP components Data access	Disclosure or betrayal of company secrets, industrial espionage, economic sabotage	Classification of data protection requirements, solutions blacklists, data reduced reports and forms
User permissions levels	Harmful data inputs	Role-based ERP apps, special mobile user accounts

At the first stage the feasibility of the designed access solution needs to be assessed. This feasibility check estimates the prospects of success of the solution considering the anticipated advantages and disadvantages. Without knowledge of the security controls actually used, the solvability of the security problems can be estimated only very vaguely.

The mobility transformations of the ERP access aim to increase defined mobility levels for the typical mobility aspects. The increase in the mobility levels generates certain security threats and vulnerabilities. Relevant security threats of mobile accesses are described in many publications [2–4, 6, 7, 11, 12, 26–28]. To determine the security vulnerabilities of each transformation, these threats have to be broken down by mobility aspects. The vulnerabilities in turn require special security controls (Table 2).

The increased requirements imply additions to the extensive security controls [26], which are already common for infrastructures that include stationary computing devices exclusively. The controls selection is intimately connected with the second stage of the feasibility check. This assessment estimates the residual security risks in detail. It decides on the final approval of the new access concept.

4 Feasibility of a Security Controls Based Mobile ERP Access

A feasibility check used in combination with security analysis should also consider technical, operational, economic, social, ethical and legal aspects [29]. Accordingly, it likewise uncovers the prospects for success of access transformations in several perspectives. It estimates whether the security controls

- are suitable to achieve confidentiality, availability, integrity and other security objectives sufficiently (technical and operational feasibility),
- comply with relevant legal and organizational regulations (legal feasibility),
- effect the intended benefits of mobility and acceptable disadvantages (economic feasibility),
- can be financed (financial feasibility),
- consider the corporate culture (cultural feasibility),
- can be adequately mastered by the company (administrative feasibility),
- are suitable to be implemented properly by the staff (human resources feasibility).

Numerous publications (e.g. [2–4, 6, 11, 15, 26, 28, 31]) comprise descriptions of several criteria that may be used to check the expected impact of defined safeguards and countermeasures for mobile access solutions. The Fig. 2 summarizes important main criteria and illustrates their relationships.

The expected level of security is calculated by a risk assessment [26, 30]. For risk acceptance, risk tolerance of the company acts as critical value [30]. The available security budget influences the acceptance of the expense of security controls. In order to verify the feasibility of a mobile ERP access solution, criteria for assessing the maturity of security management are also suitable [31]. The evidence has been furnished if the transformation effect fulfills the requirements of all the criteria listed. Best Practices, benchmarking, advice from experts and pilot experiments are helpful for assessing.

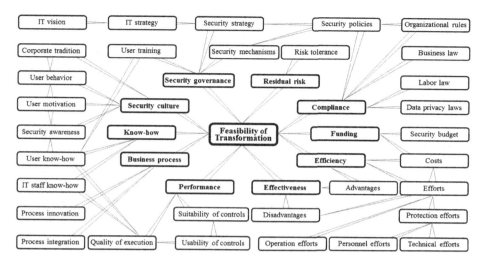

Fig. 2. Important feasibility check criteria of security controls for ERP access transformations

Based on evidence of feasibility, the company launches into a project to implement the technical and organizational conditions for the mobile access solution. The subsequent rollout of the solution can be done gradually and include a pilot project (study) with a strongly limited user base [13, 28]. A regular performance and risk monitoring [30] detects occurring security vulnerabilities and evaluates the resulting security risk. In response to the review, the options for action are: tolerate, avoid, mitigate, share or transfer the risk [30]. Risk avoidance means to reject the access solution. Risk mitigation and risk sharing over and over again requires selecting appropriate safeguards and countermeasures but also the assessment of their feasibility. Reduced security risks but also a step-up of the company's risk tolerance justify the use of more flexible access scenarios.

Risk-mitigating security controls for ERP access transformations are primarily a part of the categories

- Enhancement or replacement or better implementation of technical, organizational or user-oriented controls
- Scope reduction by shortening of whitelists [20] or enlargement of blacklists for access locations, device models, users, business applications etc.

A software that is installed and runs on users' computers (on-premises software) can be, for example, replaced by a cloud solution. Such software as a service solutions are offered for mobile device management (MDM), for mobile application management (MAM), for mobile information management (MIM), for enterprise mobility management (EMM) or for ERP systems [15, 23]. Thereby, the company reduces its own protection efforts. It often achieves improved safeguards. At the same time the company exposes itself to new security threats that are caused by the cloud concept. It shares the security risk also with the outsourcing provider. However, the partner often finds reasons to deny the compensation of occurring harms [26]. The greatest impulse for enhanced security of the mobile ERP access will be an outcome of the prospective ERP software offerings. Presumably they will contain mature mobility solutions [17, 22, 23, 32]. These solutions will include security countermeasures as integrated or combined software components.

5 Conclusion

The classification approach for mobile accesses to ERP systems enables a differentiated identification of mobility levels which have been previously achieved or which are desired. It can also be used as a basis for benchmarking [31], for the definition of security patterns [24] or for "best practices" [13, 16]. When deciding on mobile access transformations, the specific additional security risks are considered by the security analysis model with two-stage feasibility checks. The model complements the gradual concepts of Basole & Rouse [5], Krybus [7], Patel [15] and Kohne et al. [28]. Relevant main criteria for the feasibility checks of the security solutions can be derived from the introduced criteria relationship chart which supports the compilation of hierarchical checklists. Important influencing factors of the feasibility are the desired mobility goals, the risk tolerance, the security budget as well as the level of security management maturity and the level of the ERP system usage.

In a further research, it is to clarify the question: how should enterprises integrate the presented conceptual suggestions in the selection and in the configuration of prospective ERP solutions? This regards both on-premises solutions and cloud solutions. In future, included standard functions of security countermeasures will facilitate the feasibility checks. But they can only cover a portion of the safeguarding tasks. Other tasks, such as creating the security guidelines and the security-related agreements with providers of software and services must continue to assume the ERP users. Therefore, the emphasis of the security analysis will shift to the administrative, cultural and human resources domains of feasibility. This means to inspect whether the guidelines and the agreements are formulated appropriately and are adequately taken into account in the configuration of the EMM software as well as by the actions of the users and of the IT specialists.

References

1. Krannich, D.: Mobile System Design. Books on Demand, Norderstedt (2010)
2. Christmann, S.: Mobiles Internet im Unternehmenskontext. Dissertation, Universitätsverlag, Göttingen (2012)
3. Michl, B.: Chancen und risiken von mobile ERP. In: Amberg, M., Lang, M. (eds.) Innovation durch Smartphone & Co., pp. 71–102. Symposon Publishing, Düsseldorf (2011)
4. Disterer, G., Kleiner, C.: Mobile Endgeräte im Unternehmen. Springer, Heidelberg (2014)
5. Basole, R.C., Rouse, W.B.: Mobile enterprise readiness and transformation. In: Taniar, D. (ed.) Encyclopedia of Mobile Computing and Commerce, pp. 481–486. Information Science Reference, Hershey (2007)

6. Petrovic, O., Harnisch, M., Puchleitner, T.: Anforderungen an mobile applikationen: akzeptanzbestimmende faktoren. In: Gronau, N., Fohrholz, C. (eds.) Wirtschaftliche Geschäftsprozesse Durch Mobile ERP-Systeme, pp. 51–94. GITO-Verlag, Berlin (2011)

7. Krybus, I.: Transformationsstrategie für mobile business. In: Amberg, M., Lang, M. (eds.) Innovation durch Smartphone & Co., pp. 329–356. Symposion Publishing, Düsseldorf (2011)

8. Liebhart, D.: Anspruchsvolle mobile arbeiter fordern interne IT heraus. In: Computerwoche 21/2013, p. 19 (2013)

9. Homann, M.: Endbenutzer-Entwicklung mobiler ERP-Applikationen durch den Einsatz eines domänenspezifischen Entwicklungswerkzeuges. Dissertation, TU München (2014)

10. Bliem-Ritz, D.: Wearable Computing: Benutzerschnittstellen zum Anziehen. disserta Verlag, Hamburg (2014)

11. BITKOM (eds.): Bring Your Own Device. Leitfaden, Berlin (2013). www.bitkom.org/ Bitkom/Publikationen/Publikation_3046.html

12. Australian Government (eds.): Risk Management of Enterprise Mobility including Bring Your Own Device (BYOD) (2013). www.asd.gov.au/publications/protect/enterprise_mobility_bring_your_own_device_byod_paper.htm

13. Werner, M.: Konzept einer Handlungsbedarfsanalyse zur Vervollkommnung der Informationssicherheitslösung in Unternehmen am Beispiel einer BYOD-Lösung. Unveröffentlichte Bachelorthesis, HS Pforzheim (2015)

14. Abdavi, A.: Mobiles ERP: apps bringen nicht allen was. In: Computerwelt, vol. 2, p. 29 (2015)

15. Patel, R.: Enterprise Mobility Strategy & Solutions. Partridge Publishing, Gurgaon (2014)

16. Magdas, F.: MBI-Lösungen - Vergleich, Auswahl und Umsetzung am Beispiel einer MS-SQL-Server-Anbindung. Unveröffentlichte Bachelorthesis, HS Pforzheim (2013)

17. Maurer, J.: Mobile ERP: Das bieten die Hersteller. In: Computerwoche, 05 August 2015. www.computerwoche.de/a/mobile-erp-das-bieten-die-hersteller,3213240

18. Auer, D., Draheim, D., Geist, V., Kopetzky, T., Küng, J., Natschläger, C.: Towards a framework and platform for mobile distributed workflow enactment services on a possible future of ERP infrastructure. In: Piazolo, F., Felderer, M. (eds.) Innovation and Future of Enterprise Information Systems. LNISO, vol. 4, pp. 201–215. Springer, Heidelberg (2013)

19. Van Leeuwen, D.: Bring your own software. Netw. Secur. **2014**(3), 12–13 (2014)

20. Lee, J., Lee, Y., Kim, S.-C.: A white-list based security architecture (WLSA) for the safe mobile office in the BYOD era. In: Park, J.J., Arabnia, H.R., Kim, C., Shi, W., Gil, J.-M. (eds.) Grid and Pervasive Computing. LNCS, vol. 7861, pp. 860–865. Springer, Heidelberg (2013)

21. Teuteberg, F., Hilker, J., Kurbel, K.: Anwendungsschwerpunkte im Mobile Enterprise Resource Planning. In: Pousttchi, K., Turowski, K. (eds.) Mobile Commerce - Anwendungen und Perspektiven. LNI, vol. P-25, pp. 12–26. Köllen, Bonn (2003)

22. Buchner, M.: ERP-Tools aus dem App Store. In: Computerwoche, 25 November 2013. www.computerwoche.de/a/erp-tools-aus-dem-app-store,2537780

23. Gelogo, Y.E., Haeng-Kon, K.: Mobile integrated enterprise resource planning system architecture. IJCA **7**(3), 379–388 (2014)

24. Schumacher, M., Fernandez-Buglioni, E., Hybertson, D., Buschmann, F., Sommerlad, P.: Security Patterns: Integrating Security and Systems Engineering. Wiley, Chichester (2006)

25. Yoshioka, N., Washizaki, H., Maruyama, K.: A survey on security patterns. Prog. Inf. **5**, 35–47 (2008)

26. BSI (eds.): Übersicht BSI-Themen. www.bsi.bund.de/DE/Themen/themen_node.html

27. Brand, J., Kruger-Van Renen, W., Rudman, R.: Proposed practices to mitigate significant mobility security risks. IBER **14**(1), 199–219 (2015)

28. Kohne, A., Ringleb, S., Yücel, C.: Bring your own Device. Springer, Wiesbaden (2015)
29. Raggad, B.: Information Security Management. CRC Press, Boca Raton (2010)
30. NIST (eds.): Managing Information Security Risk. NIST Special Publication 800–39 (2011)
31. Campbell, G.: Measuring and Communicating Security's Value: A Compendium of Metrics for Enterprise Protection. Elsevier, Amsterdam (2015)
32. Dospinescu, O., Fotache, D., Munteanu, B.A., Hurbean, L.: Mobile enterprise resource planning: new technology horizons. CIBIMA 1(11), 91–97 (2008)

Vertical Integration and Adaptive Services in Networked Production Environments

Dennis Christmann[1]([✉]), Andreas Schmidt[2], Christian Giehl[3], Max Reichardt[1],
Moritz Ohmer[4], Markus Berg[3], Karsten Berns[1], Reinhard Gotzhein[1],
and Thorsten Herfet[2]

[1] University of Kaiserslautern, Kaiserslautern, Germany
{christma,c_giehl,reichardt,berns,gotzhein}@cs.uni-kl.de
[2] Telecommunications Lab, Saarland University, Saarbrücken, Germany
{schmidt,herfet}@nt.uni-saarland.de
[3] proAlpha Software GmbH, Weilerbach, Germany
Markus.Berg@proalpha.de
[4] DFKI Kaiserslautern, Kaiserslautern, Germany
Moritz.Ohmer@dfki.de

Abstract. A major task in the context of Industry 4.0 is the vertical integration of the layers of automation and information technology to make today's structures in production plants more flexible. While the necessity of such a step is easy to see from an administrative perspective, the technical realization is difficult, since it requires emergent software systems and implies the coupling of heterogeneous systems with different technological constraints. In this paper, we present an approach to realize this step. It is based on the coupling of adaptive components and services, which range from the field level to the management level and include wireless sensor networks, autonomous robots, and multimedia systems for remote maintenance, with an ERP system. By presenting the application in a demonstration production plant bottling liquid soap, we provide evidence of the approach's economical and technological benefits.

1 Introduction

The objective of Industry 4.0 is to improve the efficiency of the production process with respect to costs, resource management, administration, and maintenance effort by enhancing the "smartness" of production plants as well as their components. In this regard, a major precondition is to make today's structures in production environments more flexible. This requires the vertical integration of the layers of automation (AT) and information technology (IT), and the development and usage of emergent software systems. By this means, heterogeneous systems and components can be coupled, and production processes can be monitored and controlled more adaptively and in a fine-grained way, since direct access from the management and ERP (Enterprise Resource Planning) layer to components as well as properties of the field and control layer becomes possible.

© Springer International Publishing Switzerland 2016
M. Felderer et al. (Eds.): ERP Future 2015 - Research, LNBIP 245, pp. 147–162, 2016.
DOI: 10.1007/978-3-319-32799-0_12

In this paper, we show results providing such fundamental foundations of Industry 4.0. We, particularly, summarize an approach to couple the proALPHA[1] ERP system with physical sensors of the plant, which are provided with real-time guarantees in terms of distributed services that are adaptive with respect to quality-of-service (QoS) and provided on demand. By optionally aggregating these services, flexible monitoring of production process parameters becomes possible and disturbances can be detected quickly. Furthermore, this paper presents the integration of autonomous mobile service robots and a networked multimedia system into the production process and the ERP system, which simplifies remote maintenance essentially and reduces downtimes. Thereby, the advantages of decomposing the static structures of today's production environments and of vertical integration in networked production plants within the AT level and across its borders is illustrated by means of concrete examples.

The core of our solution consists of a QoS-capable middleware concept for production plants. Though the solution composes several heterogeneous middleware systems, which are specialized with respect to their application purpose and corresponding requirements (e.g., a middleware for multimedia systems or a novel middleware for wireless sensor networks (WSNs) with real-time constraints), their interfaces are generic and follow the idea of emergent software to enable a seamless and systematical integration of the AT and IT worlds.

The results presented in this paper are the results of a research project, which was supported by the German Federal Ministry of Education and Research within Task 6.1.4 "Adaptive Services in Networked Production Environments" of the joint project SINNODIUM[2] (Software Innovations for the Digital Enterprise) between 2013 and 2015. In the paper, we outline developed components and middlewares (Sect. 2), which are necessary for the provision of services with QoS guarantees and the vertical integration of production processes. Furthermore, we present the demonstrator VI-P (Sect. 3), in which the components have been integrated into an existing production plant bottling liquid soap. The paper is supplemented by a survey on related work (Sect. 4) and a conclusion (Sect. 5).

2   Vertical Integration of Production Processes

The overall architecture showing the components and their relationships is illustrated in Fig. 1. The figure also presents the integration of the ERP system and its interaction with other components. The wireless sensors are distributed in the production plant (mobile or stationary), whereas service robots are mobile and navigate autonomously. The networked multimedia system has full access to all services provided by the production plant and, in particular, also to the service robots. Since parts of the multimedia system can be located in a place different from the production plant, remote maintenance supported by monitoring services of the plant and service robots is possible. More details on each component are given in the following subsections.

---

[1] http://www.proalpha.de.

[2] http://www.software-cluster.com/en/research/projects/joint-projects/.

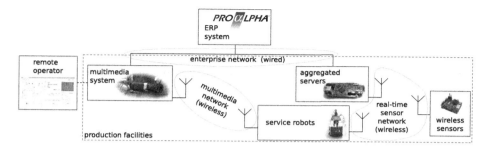

Fig. 1. Components of an enterprise's infrastructure with vertical integration.

2.1   The Role of the ERP System

As a software provider for mid-sized enterprises, the proALPHA Software GmbH has always been a lead in empowering sophisticated working environments by incorporating a multi-tier software system tailored to customer needs. As industry requirements and technical opportunities advance rapidly, so does the information density [1]. Too much information blurs the decision-making process and all the worse yields errors [2]. Targeting profound decisions, managing directors need a comprehensive view on both the business and manufacturing process levels. Thus, the main target regarding vertical integration is connecting a high-level IT system with low-level machinery interfaces. This approach enables I/O operations on low-level machine data, which is achieved in the ERP system by using the OPC UA (OPC Unified Architecture) protocol stack[3] in connection with the proALPHA workflow lifecycle for high-level business steering.

The incorporated proALPHA module is based on the generation of KPIs (Key Performance Indicators), which are defined using mathematical formulas on machine input values, e.g., the ratio of produced and broken pieces. To do so, the first task was to create an interface that can perform basic I/O operations on the production plant data interfaces, which are usually highly heterogeneous and specific to the hardware manufacturer [1]. Being the most flexible communication technology available, the OPC UA protocol has been integrated into the proALPHA codebase. Having this basic operations available in the API (Application Programming Interface), the data can be processed further within the proALPHA ERP. Hence, the proALPHA user can build up a dynamic rule catalog using operator blocks and propositional logic, which then triggers and steers standard proALPHA workflows. Some implemented operator blocks can be found in Table 1. With these, more sophisticated rules can be built, e.g., a temperature check returning a boolean (see Algorithm 1). A typical example of how machine data can enhance business workflow logic is to put a lock on a certain production order as soon as an error is detected within a critical part of the production plant (see Algorithm 2).

---

[3] see [3] or https://opcfoundation.org/.

Table 1. Atomic operator blocks which can be used for creating higher-order operator blocks.

Operator block	Description
greaterThan(*value*, params)	evaluates to true iff. all values in params are greater than *value*
lessThan(*value*, params)	evaluates to true iff. all values in params are less than *value*
alwaysTrue()	returns always true, e.g., if a proALPHA workflow should be triggered every time a data change is detected
equals(*value*, params)	evaluates to true iff. all params are equal to *value*

Algorithm 1. Aggregation of atomic blocks to build a higher-order GOODTEMPERATURE block.

```
1: procedure GOODTEMPERATURE(value)
2:     return greaterThan(value, 40) AND lessThan(value, 130)
3: end procedure
```

Algorithm 2. ProALPHA workflow trigger based on GOODTEMPERATURE block.

```
   procedure CHECKTEMPERATUREDATA(value)
2:     if NOT goodTemperature(value) then
           trigger proALPHA workflow"lock production"
4:         trigger proALPHA workflow"maintenance &repair"
       end if
6: end procedure
```

Another challenge that had to be met was to find a suitable presentation and abstraction of machine data with respect to information flow. As said, the information density is increasing and a suitable information-preserving abstraction is still a matter of research. This especially holds for the majority of mid-sized industry environments where IT systems are still widely homogeneous and inflexible with partly old-fashioned interfaces, the target customer group for the proALPHA Software GmbH. Being a research interest for both industrial and academic partners, the interfaces need to be modern and flexible while still being able to access real-time data provided by the ERP system. To promote a contemporary flexibility, the presentation is done by a slim browser application (see Sect. 2.5). This application takes the information directly from a RESTful (REpresentational State Transfer) interface, also provided by the proALPHA ESB (Enterprise Service Bus), which exports any information held by the ERP. Regarding the workflow logic, this interface ultimately notifies the browser application that a state changed and provides machine data for the user to interact.

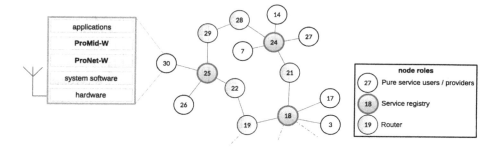

Fig. 2. Network topology with overlay structure of *ProMid-W*.

2.2   Monitoring of Production Processes with Real-Time Guarantees

To monitor and control parameters of the production process, WSNs are an attractive solution due to their flexible application and falling prices. However, many plants have special demands with respect to QoS – in particular, regarding reliability and delays –, which are satisfied insufficiently by existing communication standards such as WirelessHART [4]. To meet these demands, two novel components have been devised to run a wireless real-time sensor network: *ProMid-W*, a QoS-capable middleware for production environments, and *ProNet-W*, a real-time-capable protocol stack for WSNs. Since they are both designed for networks consisting of nodes with scarce hardware resources, efficiency and the reduction of overhead were one of the main objectives in the design. Both components have been implemented in C++ for the Imote2 sensor platform[4] and ns-3[5].

ProMid-W (Production Middleware – Wireless) is a service-oriented middleware for production environments with partial mobility. A service of *ProMid-W* can provide either measured sensor values (e.g., a temperature) or logical values (e.g., status of a pump), where both event- and time-triggered services are supported. Services are addressed by a logical identifier and described by QoS parameters (e.g., the minimal interval in which the service can be provided) and a type (e.g., stationary temperature sensor). *ProMid-W*'s mode of operation follows a publish/subscribe pattern, where a service is first published by the service provider and possibly subscribed by service users with a desired QoS afterwards.

The announcement and discovery of services is done with the help of a distributed registry storing information about available services. For this purpose, *ProMid-W* puts an overlay structure on the network, which is, technically spoken, constructed by a clustering algorithm building a 3-hop connected 1-hop dominating set. This algorithm uses information about the network topology, which is provided by the Automatic Topology Discovery Protocol [5]. As illustrated in Fig. 2, *ProMid-W* distinguishes three types of nodes: First, pure service

---

[4] http://vs.cs.uni-kl.de/downloads/Imote2NET_ED_Datasheet.pdf.
[5] http://www.nsnam.org.

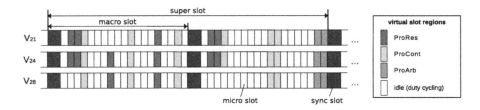

Fig. 3. Medium slotting in *ProNet-W*.

users and providers; second, service registry nodes, which store available services and are consulted when particular services are searched; and third, router nodes, which forward messages in the overlay network. The algorithm determining the type of a node is configurable, where the selection of a node as registry node or router can be enforced or excluded. Thereby, limitations of nodes are taken into account and energy resources of battery-powered nodes can be preserved.

The protocol stack *ProNet-W* (Production Network – Wireless) is a software component for the wireless interconnection of sensor and actuator nodes and is utilized by *ProMid-W*. It includes the synchronization protocol *Black Burst Synchronization* (BBS, [6]) providing low and bounded synchronization offset and several real-time MAC (Medium Access Control) protocols like a TDMA-based (Time Division Multiple Access) protocol with exclusive reservations. Based on BBS, *ProNet-W* subdivides time into *micro*, *macro*, and *super slots* (see Fig. 3): Micro slots are the smallest time unit and can be grouped into so-called *virtual slot regions*, which define the active MAC protocol for a particular range of micro slots. If no MAC protocol is specified explicitly, *ProNet-W* disables the transceiver, thereby making duty cycling an inherent part of *ProNet-W*. Macro slots consist of a configurable number of micro slots and define the interval of resynchronization. Super slots comprise a configurable number of macro slots and define the interval on which the pattern of virtual slot regions recur.

Besides the TDMA-based protocol that is, in particular, attractive if data is sent periodically, *ProNet-W* also includes a CSMA-based (Carrier Sense Multiple Access) protocol if no guarantees are required and the *Arbitrating and Cooperative Transfer Protocol* resolving contest deterministically by means of strict priorities [7]. Due to the diverseness of these protocols and their flexible application within one scenario, *ProNet-W* builds an adequate foundation for a wide range of applications with and without stringent QoS constraints.

2.3 Orchestration and Aggregation of Services

The biggest challenge of vertical integration is to bridge the technological gap between the IT layer, in which simplicity and flexibility are essential, and the AT layer, where real-time constraints and devices with low hardware resources are predominant. Our solution tackles this challenge by so-called *aggregated servers*, which act as gateway between various communication technologies (see Fig. 1).

Aggregated servers represent an abstraction layer between the IT layer and production services on field level, which are provided by PLCs (Programmable

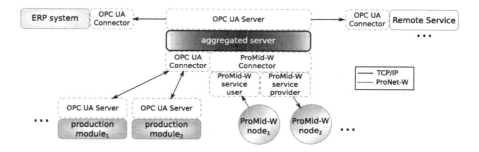

Fig. 4. An *aggregated server* and its interfaces.

Logic Controllers) using the OPC UA protocol stack and wireless sensor nodes running ProMid-W/ProNet-W (see Sect. 2.2), respectively. The *aggregated servers* are responsible for the orchestration of the field level services and the collection of their data. The services and their data are merged into a uniform semantical information model based on OPC UA, where KPIs are generated on the basis of the model and standardized KPI templates (ISO 22400[6]). These KPIs are homogeneous and machine-readable and have a uniform semantical description to make them accessible and processable by business applications such as ERP systems. In this regard, data of services are already aggregated on field level to accommodate the increasing data volumes of Industry 4.0, and failure KPIs are generated to enable the detection of problems in the production process on IT level. The information model is enhanced by additional semantical descriptions, which associate the KPIs with their origin in the production plant.

The architecture of *aggregated servers* is presented by Fig. 4. Each *aggregated server* has an OPC UA connector to access data provided by OPC UA servers in the production plant, a ProMid-W connector to use/provide services in the WSN, and an OPC UA server as uplink to business applications. Due to their proximity to the field level, where hardware with scarce resources are common, *aggregated servers* run on embedded platforms[7].

2.4   Integration of Service Robots

A promising area for research and novel applications is the homogeneous integration of mobile service robots into the service network of production facilities. Robots such as Automated Guided Vehicles (AGVs) can provide services that make facility operation more flexible, safer, and economically viable. In the remote maintenance context of this project, realized robot services include safe navigation to target positions, direct teleoperation, as well as access to robot sensor data and system states. Apart from providing services, it is advantageous if robots also use suitable services available in the production plant. This way, robots may operate more efficiently or possibly less sensors are required on the

---

[6] http://www.iso.org/iso/catalogue_detail.htm?csnumber=54497.

[7] In VI-P (see Sect. 3), the Aria G25 (http://www.acmesystems.it/aria) is used.

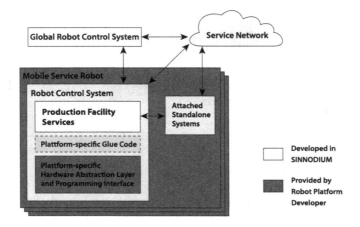

Fig. 5. Overview on the robot control software.

robot platforms. The latter has significant advantages with respect to costs. Further advantages include reduced size and energy consumption. In the scope of this project, sensor data provided by wireless sensor nodes and an external localization service was processed to improve navigation.

To achieve the goals, a flexible and extensible software component (*"Production Facility Services"*) suitable for multiple robot platforms was developed. It provides and uses services in the production network (see Fig. 1). Figure 5 illustrates the component in its closer context. The robot platform and its application programming interface (API) are provided by the developer of the robot platform. Platform-specific glue code bridges the API to the *Production Facility Services* component. The *Global Robot Control System* coordinates multiple robots and provides services independent of a specific robot. Apart from that, standalone networked systems can flexibly be attached to robot platforms.

Figure 6 shows the component's coarse structure. The APIs of robot platforms have major differences: While some already provide functionality for autonomous navigation, other platforms are controlled by specifying current velocities. Autonomous navigation typically requires sub-components for localization, mapping, and path planning. All three tasks can be optimized using services available in the production network. A component group for autonomous navigation is therefore a central part of the developed solution. Implemented in a modular way, sub-components may be replaced by platform-specific functionality already provided by the robot API. On top, an extensible set of sub-components implements the actual robot services.

The implementation is based on the robotics software framework Finroc[8] [8]. The component is composed from interconnected sub-components. Their interfaces consist of a set of ports, as common in robot control systems. It is always possible to realize application-specific bridges between the production network

---

[8] http://finroc.org.

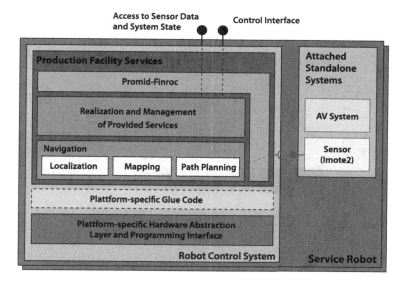

Fig. 6. Coarse structure of components on service robots.

and such ports – typically in dedicated sub-components. Generic solutions, however, have advantages with respect to quality attributes such as interoperability, maintainability, and flexibility [9]. Thus, the *ProMid-Finroc* plugin provides the required middleware such as *OPC UA* and *ProMid-W* and enables generic interconnectability with ports.

2.5 Remote Maintenance

With more and more production sites being outsourced, it is no longer possible to provide the same coverage with support technicians and engineers as with all sites inside one country or continent. Even today, in a world where everyone is connected to a global network that allows nearly instant communication, it is still necessary that engineers travel abroad and that there are highly specialized workforces on-site that ensure proper operation of these plants.

By providing web-based multimedia applications with convenient collaboration mechanisms, it becomes possible that experts can stay in their home country and supervise the local workers remotely. With remote maintenance, a single technician working in Central Europe can quickly switch between sites, e.g., maintaining a production system in India in the morning, confirming a false alarm in Brazil before lunch, and handling a power recovery in South Africa in the afternoon.

To support this use case, we have developed a networked multimedia system (cp. Fig. 1) internally consisting of two independent components, namely *ReMain Net* and *ReMain Dashboard*, which interact closely with other components such as the ERP system and the service robot (see Fig. 7). The *ReMain* components

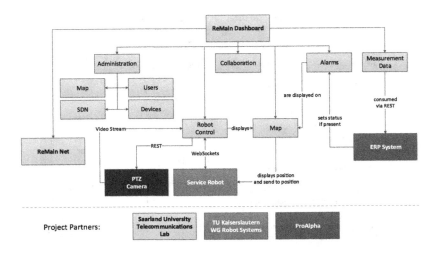

Fig. 7. *ReMain* components and interaction with others.

provide foundations for efficient WAN (Wide Area Network) communication and implement a web-based monitoring application for managing production plants.

ReMain Net is an instantiation of the new paradigm *Software Defined Networking* (SDN) [10]. It offers new possibilities in terms of network monitoring and orchestration, by decoupling the data plane from the control plane. The core of such a network is a central controller instance, which is responsible for routing tasks, thus implementing the control plane. Being open source software and no proprietary hardware/software implementation, it is highly flexible. As remote maintenance requires efficient multimedia transport, this network architecture opens opportunities to optimize the transport using different mechanisms.

The controller software of *ReMain Net* is based on *Floodlight*[9], which is written in *Java*. The original implementation has been extended by several features, including on-demand changes to the routing metric or extensive gathering of network statistics [11]. Furthermore, it includes a means to manage so-called *Relays*. We found out that the traditional end-to-end principle present in today's networks is often not optimal and performance can be improved by transparently terminating a connection on the path between communicating peers [12]. The controller can instrument these relays and adapt the transmission appropriately.

ReMain Dashboard provides a web-based graphical user interface to production site engineers and local operators. By using state-of-the-art open source web frameworks, the application can be used on a variety of operating systems without any licensing fees. The backend can be installed on all systems where *Node.js*[10] is available, while the frontend requires a modern browser. The application includes collaboration mechanisms that allow multiple users to communicate via video and audio, while using the dashboard and handling incidents.

---

[9] http://www.projectfloodlight.org/floodlight/.
[10] https://nodejs.org/.

This enables, for instance, a remote expert to supervise a local operator during maintenance, using an audio connection between the two. During the process, the expert can monitor system parameters and can quickly react upon changes, by advising his on-site co-worker. The requirement for a local operator can even be removed by using a service robot, since the applications can steer the robot and its camera. The included map of the site shows the robot's position as well as the locations of other components such as sensors and cameras.

Alarms, which are indicated by information from the ERP system, are also visible through the interface. The relevant sensor is highlighted on the map and as soon as the problem is fixed, a resolution can be entered. This note is archived, so that recurring problems can be identified and resolved faster. Finally, there is a complete administration section for managing user accounts, connection parameters, and device details.

3   The VI-P Demonstrator

All components described in Sect. 2 have been integrated in the VI-P (Vertical Integration of Production Processes) demonstrator, which is located in the Living Lab $SmartFactory^{KL}$ and shows the advantages of vertical integration and emergent software in an example production plant bottling liquid colored soap.[11] In this plant, the following fault situation is considered exemplarily: During the production of colored soap, a pump fails (simulated by a hardware switch). This failure has to be detected in real-time and stored in a failure variable, which is monitored by the ERP system. To reduce downtime, the detection of the failure automatically starts a workflow to identify the particular source of the fault and to start repairing. A specialist is consulted in form of a remote maintenance job, as it is not economical or possible to have a specialist on standby on-site, in particular, if the production site is small or outlying. To begin with, this specialist has to get a first impression of the problem. On this, he orders a mobile service robot, which is equipped with a multimedia system, to the faulty pump and evaluates the video streams of the robot. After identifying the source of the problem, a local technician is consulted, who repairs the faulty pump while being guided by the remote specialist.

To handle this scenario, the integrated components interact as follows: The start is triggered by a *ProMid-W* service (see Sect. 2.2), which monitors the status of the pump and notifies of its deficiency and position in the plant. Beside this pump status, several other *ProMid-W* services such as temperature and gas sensors are installed in the plant. The failure of the pump is transmitted via *ProNet-W*, which realizes the real-time sensor network consisting of six Imote2 in the scenario, to an *aggregated server* (see Sect. 2.3). Physically, this *aggregated server* interconnects an Imote2 and an Aria G25 platform via a serial line by a so-called SmartBoard (see Fig. 8), which is connected to the enterprise network

---

[11] Videos of the demonstrator are available at http://vs.informatik.uni-kl.de/activities/ Sinnodium/ and http://www.software-cluster-portal.de/innovationsDetail.php?ID= ID3220_346405773.

Fig. 8. Hardware in VI-P: the SmartBoard interconnecting an Imote2 and an Aria G25 (top left), the *ReMain* hardware setup including local parts of *ReMain Net* and a small Lenovo PC running the *ReMain Dashboard* (bottom left), and the service robot (right).

via a LAN interface. On the software side, stub implementations are provided for the Imote2 and Aria G25 platforms to bridge the gap between real-time sensor network and enterprise network. Via these stubs, the *aggregated server* has full access to the services provided by *ProMid-W*.

The *aggregated server* transforms the data provided by *ProMid-W*, i.e., also the detected fault, into KPIs and provides these values via OPC UA, thereby making *ProMid-W* services available in the enterprise network. The ERP system subscribed to these OPC UA services receives a data-change event and consumes the new data value. The value is evaluated by a user-defined set of evaluation rules based on propositional logic terms and processed by the ERP system within a predefined business logic workflow. In this scenario, the ERP system triggers a workflow to suspend the production process and to inform a remote operator via the *ReMain Dashboard*. This approach connects the raw plant data with enterprise logic while still providing filtering mechanisms to reduce data volume.

After indication of the pump failure, the *ReMain Dashboard* (see Sect. 2.5) gets updated and highlights the affected plant on the overview page. The operator can then click on the site to see more details, such as system parameters and component states (see Fig. 9), and to locate the fault. By using the robot control module, he can order the service robot to drive to the desired location. While driving and at the fault position, the camera on the robot can be tilted, panned, and zoomed to get a better view on the situation. The remote expert can collaborate with a local operator using audio and video streams inside the web interface. Thereby, both share a view on the plant, including important parameters such as temperatures and quality rates. The resolution of the fault

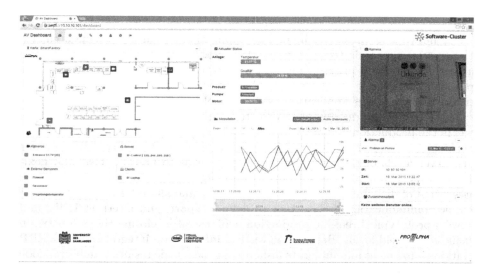

Fig. 9. The *ReMain Dashboard*: visualization of production variables, remote maintenance, and interaction with service robots.

can finally be entered into a alarm database, for future reference when similar problems arise.

The software components for mobile robots (see Sect. 2.4) were instantiated on the mobile indoor platform Marvin (see Fig. 8) [13]. They were configured for platform, environment, and application scenario. In the demonstrator setup, an audio/video system as well as a wireless sensor node were attached to the robot platform. Furthermore, the *ReMain Dashboard* was also installed on the robot's touch screen. This way, local staff can see the current state of a component in the plant. Apart from that, it allows hands-free illustrations as well as visual telephony. Since mobile robots may not always enter all areas of production plants – e.g., in case of gas leaks or extreme temperatures –, the robot subscribes to all relevant sensor services along planned routes. If critical sensor values are received – like in the scenario, from a *ProMid-W* service simulating a gas leak –, the robot automatically plans a different safe route to the desired target position.

4   Related Work

In literature, many related work can be found on each integrated component. However, in this paper, we limit the discussion to approaches with vertical integration and the coupling of ERP systems with service robots and WSNs.

In the service robot domain, commercially available AGVs for intralogistics are regularly coupled to ERP systems in industrial applications. There are various companies providing such vehicles and integration services – e.g., Swisslog, MLR or psb intralogistics[12]. We are, however, not aware of any project

---

[12] http://www.swisslog.com, http://www.mlr.de, http://www.psb-gmbh.de.

integrating autonomous mobile systems in a vertically integrated production service network as presented here. The application scenario – telemaintenance of industrial sites – is topic of other dedicated research projects such as the current MainTelRob project [14], which involves an industry robot arm. Our approach, however, focuses on vertical integration – utilizing existing generic services to realize this application as an example.

Since modern production plants create a high amount of output data on each level of the production domain, business level IT systems need to be directly connected to the several levels to make optimal decisions. Coupling ERP systems with lower levels of the automation pyramid needs to be easy, fast, and flexible, allowing heterogeneous systems to be integrated. A first step towards the integration of distributed IT systems is to define and share KPIs. [1] proposes a flexible communication architecture to define, export, and interpret KPIs, and shows a prototypical real-life production demonstrator, closing the gap between business and field levels. Besides the vertical information integration, most ERP solutions implement and integrate in-house business logic resulting in bigger code bases and high maintenance effort. Fast networks allow for outsourcing of business logic and distributed computing. [2] proposes how the alignment of intra- and inter-organizational process management can be achieved with horizontal integration and the requirements that need to be matched.

Due to technical improvements and falling prices of equipment, the integration of WSNs into ERP systems becomes increasingly popular [15, 16]. A concrete example presenting the application of WSNs in industrial context is GINSENG, which has been evaluated in a live oil refinery [17]. In this demonstrator, the deployed sensor network was used to realize wireless control loops and to monitor the production process, which is made visible by integrating GINSENG into existing ERP systems via an OSGi-based (Open Service Gateway initiative) middleware. Another demonstrator, also from the oil industry, is described in [18]. Here, the focus is on the integration of various sensor hardware platforms into one enterprise environment. Their interface to SAP ERP systems is based on the UPnP standard, which is either provided by a sensor node directly or by special gateway nodes transforming data of proprietary WSN protocols into UPnP variables. Compared to our approach, both examples have similarities with respect to the transformation of sensor data, but rely on different standards (OSGi/UPnP vs. OPC UA).

5 Conclusions

In this paper, we have presented an approach for the vertical integration of the AT and IT layers. It is based on a QoS-capable middleware concept, which couples services and components of the field level with the management level and ERP systems. In particular, our integration incorporates the following components: ERP software systems provided by the proAlpha Software GmbH, WSNs with real-time guarantees monitoring the production process on field level, aggregated servers acting as gateways between the WSNs and the enterprise network, autonomous mobile service robots, and multimedia systems. In summary, the resulting integrated system has following contributions:

- Services are provided with QoS and enable the monitoring of production processes with real-time guarantees.
- The realized middleware concept outperforms existing solutions with respect to flexibility and adaptivity, since services can be subscribed on demand and with the QoS they need.
- The presented remote maintenance process supported by a multimedia system and service robots improves repair measures and decreases downtimes.

To show the feasibility and benefits of our integration approach, all components have been instantiated in a real production plant bottling liquid soap. In this plant, a failure of a pump was triggered to demonstrate the use and interaction of all components. In particular, the use case illustrated how the collaboration of the components reported the fault, identified its source, and provided support for remote maintenance to assist a local operator during repairing. It demonstrated that our approach is well-suited for production plants with moderate electromagnetic interference. In harsher environments with, for instance, many tremendously powerful engines, the wireless communication realized by some components may suffer from bad environmental conditions, thereby disqualifying these components and wireless technologies in general.

Acknowledgement. This work was funded by the German Federal Ministry of Education and Research (BMBF) within the joint project SINNODIUM.

References

1. Gerber, T., Bosch, H.-C., Johnsson, C.: Vertical integration of decision-relevant production information into IT systems of manufacturing companies. In: Borangiu, T., Thomas, A., Trentesaux, D. (eds.) Service Orientation in Holonic and Multi agent, SCI, vol. 472, pp. 263–278. Springer, Heidelberg (2013)
2. Wangler, B., Paheerathan, S.J.: Horizontal and vertical integration of organizational IT systems. Information Systems Engineering (2000)
3. Mahnke, W., Leitner, S.H., Damm, M.: OPC Unified Architecture, 1st edn. Springer Publishing Company Inc., Heidelberg (2009)
4. International Electrotechnical Commission: Industrial Communication Networks - Wireless Communication Network and Communication Profiles - WirelessHART (IEC 6259 1st edn. 1.0), April 2010
5. Kramer, C., Christmann, D., Gotzhein, R.: Automatic topology discovery in TDMA-based Ad Hoc networks. In: IWCMC 2015: 11th International Wireless Communications and Mobile Computing Conference, Dubrovnik, August 2015
6. Gotzhein, R., Kuhn, T.: Black burst synchronization (BBS) - a protocol for deterministic tick and time synchronization in wireless networks. Comput. Netw. **55**(13), 3015–3031 (2011)
7. Christmann, D., Gotzhein, R., Rohr, S.: The arbitrating value transfer protocol (AVTP) - deterministic binary countdown in wireless multi-hop networks. In: Computer Communications and Networks (ICCCN 2012), August 2012

8. Reichardt, M., Föhst, T., Berns, K.: On software quality-motivated design of a real-time framework for complex robot control systems. Electronic Communications of the EASST 60, August 2013. http://journal.ub.tu-berlin.de/eceasst/article/view/855

9. Reichardt, M., Föhst, T., Fleischmann, P., Arndt, M., Berns, K.: Principles in framework design applied in networked robotics. In: Proceedings of the 3rd IFAC Symposium on Telematics Applications, Seoul, November 2013

10. Nadeau, T.D., Gray, K.: SDN: Software Defined Networks, 1st edn. O'Reilly, California (2013)

11. Schmidt, A.: Network Traffic and Infrastructure Analysis in Software Defined Networks, Master Thesis, Saarland University, May 2015

12. Karl, M., Herfet, T.: Transparent multi-hop protocol termination. In: Advanced Information Networking and Applications (AINA) (2014)

13. Hillenbrand, C., Berns, K.: Modulare Sicherheits- und Sensorsysteme für autonome mobile Roboter realisiert im Forschungsfahrzeug Marvin. In: Berns, K., Luksch, T. (eds.) Autonome Mobile Systeme 2007. Informatik aktuell, pp. 133–137. Springer, Heidelberg (2007)

14. Sittner, F.C.A., Aschenbrenner, D., Fritscher, M., Kheirkhah, A., Krauss, M., Schilling, K.: Maintenance and telematics for robots (MainTelRob). In: Lee, J. (ed.) 3rd International Federation of Automatic Control IFAC Symposium on Telematics Applications, Seoul, November 11–13 (2013)

15. Gomez, L., Laube, A., Sorniotti, A.: Design guidelines for integration of wireless sensor networks with enterprise systems. In: Proceedings of the 1st International Conference on MOBILE Wireless MiddleWARE, Operating Systems, and Applications, MOBILWARE 2008. ICST, Brussels (2007)

16. Thoma, M., Sperner, K., Braun, T.: Service descriptions and linked data for integrating WSNs into enterprise IT. In: 3rd International Workshop on Software Engineering for Sensor Network Application, SESENA, Zurich, Switzerland. IEEE (2012)

17. Busching, F., Pottner, W., Brokelmann, D., von Zengen, G., Hartung, R., Hinz, K., Wolf, L.: A Demonstrator of the GINSENG-approach to performance and closed loop control in WSNs. In: 2012 Ninth International Conference on Networked Sensing Systems (INSS), June 2012

18. Marin-Perianu, M., Meratnia, N., Havinga, P.J.M., de Souza, L.M.S., Müller, J., Spiess, P., Haller, S., Riedel, T., Decker, C., Stromberg, G.: Decentralized enterprise systems: a multiplatform wireless sensor network approach. IEEE Wireless Commun. 14(6), 57 (2007)

Author Index

Printed in the United States
By Bookmasters